The Economic Rise of China

By Arthur H Tafero

Forward

When I first came to China in 2008, it appeared as if every other block of every city was under construction. There was construction everywhere and it was damned inconvenient. But, in the short span of only thirty years, China had gone from a backward third-rate economy to a flourishing economic giant that is on the verge of taking over Japan's spot as top dog in the East.

It has not been a smooth road. The environment has taken a terrible beating from unrestrained expansion of Chinese businesses on the mainland. Millions have been uprooted for the Three Gorges Dam project as well as construction of the state-of-the art Bullet Train, which far exceeds anything the United States has in public transportation. It is tough to make an omelet without breaking a few eggs.

The economy has exploded, but not without some dangerous side effects. Apartment housing costs have sky-rocketed in China's major cities. Apartments are now selling at ridiculous prices that far exceed the cost of a comfortable house in the United States. Real estate inflation, pollution, corruption and an overheated economy are just a few of the challenges that the CCP must contend with.

State-owned enterprises are on the decline. Stock markets are now trying to gain a foothold in the Chinese mainland, but face the 10% rule put in place by the CCP. If a stock goes up or down 10% in one day, trading is automatically halted until the next day; something that could never happen in the West. There is limited law enforcement, so people here generally make up their own rules as they go along in this primarily Confucian society.

The Chinese economy in the 21st century greatly resembles the Wild West of the 1880s in the United States. There was little law west of the Mississippi. That is pretty much what it is like in the 21st century in China.

You can download anything you want on the Chinese internet. Movies are free, music is free, and software is free. All of this sounds great until you find out that all the people who create these things are migrating away from China by the millions. This brain drain is a serious problem for the CCP and the issue of intellectual property protection is now being seriously considered by Beijing. China cannot afford to lag behind in tech to Japan and India, its primary competitors in Asia. Those countries have full IPP, but China does not in this point in time.

Despite all these and other problems, the Chinese economy keeps rising by almost double digits every year. The Chinese have the lowest production costs for goods in the world, primarily due to the least expensive work force in the world. Add this to the tremendous study and work ethic of the Chinese, and you have a combination that will be very difficult for any other country to beat in the near future of import and export.

This book will examine the events and changes that took place from 1949 until the present time that has launched China into a position of economic prominence in the Far East. Part Two of the book examines a SWOT analysis of China and looks at several major Chinese companies.

Arthur H Tafero

Table of Contents

Forward..1

Table of Contents...3

Part One – China in the Last Century

Chapter One: 1911 and a Country in Chaos...4

Chapter Two: 1949 and Problems Faced by Mao...9

Chapter Three: Disaster in the 1960s..14

Chapter Four: 1976; The Death of Mao and the Opening Up of China Under Deng...........19

Chapter Five: The Special Economic Zones Boost China's Economy................23

Chapter Six: The Chinese Economy Eventually Prospers Under Jiang Zemin (1989-2002)...29

Chapter Seven: The Overheating of the Chinese Economy and Migration Problems............32

Chapter Eight: The Problem of IPP (Intellectual Property Protection)..................37

Chapter Nine: The Bullet Train and the Three Gorges Project............................40

Chapter Ten: The Hu Jintao Era (2002-2012) and Xi Jingping.............................45

Part Two: Current State of Affairs in China and Economic Case Studies

Chapter Eleven: A SWOT Analysis of China as of 2015......................................48

Chapter Twelve: Case Studies: Chinese Companies; Sales, Market Share and Stock Price...52

Chapter One – # 1911: A Country in Chaos

The New Republic

In 1911, China was a country in complete chaos. The Qing Dynasty had just succumbed to a number of severe setbacks including the The Opium War, The Taiping Rebellion and the Boxer Rebellion. A humiliating loss to Japan in 1896 sealed the doom of the Qing leaders. How could a country the size of China lose a war to a small island?

The answer was quite simple; Japan had progressed in technology and modern Western capitalism, while China had wallowed in the past with weapons from the eighteenth century and a complete disregard for a well-equipped navy. China was miserably behind the times.

The outlying regions of China were almost ungovernable. Tibet and Mongolia were far behind the powers of the Qing government to govern. So both regions began to govern themselves via warlords. In effect, China had lost almost one third of its territory with as the chaos of 1911 began. What would follow would be almost four unfortunate decades of warlordism, world war, and civil war.

By 1912, Sun Yat-sen was declared president of the new republic, but was immediately forced to hand over power to warlord, Yuan Shikai. Shikai tried to reinstate the imperial throne by declaring himself emperor, but failed miserably and died in disgrace in 1916.

Sun Yat-sen, the First President of the New Republic of China in 1912

Yuan Shakai, a warlord who attempted to displace Sun, but failed in 1912

After Shakai's death in 1916, a number of insignificant warlords created turmoil for the New Republic for several years. In 1919, the Versailles Treaty proved to be unfair to the Chinese, and the result was the May Fourth Movement, a violent protest in Beijing against awarding German lands in China to Japan. This movement lasted until 1921.

Concurrently, the Russian Revolution had taken place and had a profound effect on China. Leninist/Marxist philosophy began to inspire Chinese who had been under the rule of emperors and warlords for thousands of years. Marxism was the belief that power belonged to the people; not kings, emperors or warlords. Anything, including communism, was better than being under the yolk of emperors and warlords. Democracy was merely a vague concept that provided little protection against local warlords. Common Chinese people began to wonder if they could do the same thing in China that Lenin did in Russia. Power to the people had a strong attraction for commoners in China.

Lenin during the Russian Revolution of 1917

Moscow did not miss this opportunity to spread communism to China. It sent people and money to China in order to finance the first communist movement in that country in the 1920s. Sun Yat-sen and his number one general Chiang Kai-shek, began to ally themselves with the Russian communists until Sun's death in 1925. After Sun died, Chiang took control of the fledgling Republic and brought most of Southern and Central China under the control of the KMT (Kuomintang) by 1927. Chiang then turned on the CCP (Chinese Communist Party) and began a relentless pursuit of communist forces from 1928 until the eventual victory of the CCP in 1949, a period of over 20 years of turmoil.

Chiang Kai-shek, successor to Sun Yat-sen and leader of the unsuccessful KMT

The KMT chased the CCP all over China for the next seven years, as the CCP made its famous Long March and regrouped under Mao Zedong in 1935 in Yan'an in Shaanxi Province, located in the Northwest of China. Stalin offered assistance to Mao during this period and Mao would be thankful to Stalin for the next 20 years until Stalin's death and the rise of Khrushchev. Meanwhile Chiang continued his pursuit to eliminate the CCP from the scene in China.

In 1937, another complication arose in this internal conflict. The invasion of China by the Japanese would last for eight long and bitter years until the United States dropped two atom bombs on Japan in 1945. One general in the CCP said he would have dropped a hundred atom bombs on China if China had possessed them. The Japanese, during this period of occupation of China, gradually consumed almost two thirds of Chinese territory, while the KMT and the CCP were busy fighting each other and occasionally warding off the Japanese from their flanks as they retreated further into Western China. The death toll was well over ten million Chinese.

By the end of the war in 1945, the KMT began to take control of most of the major Chinese cities, and the CCP began to exert its influence on the countryside and all the territory in between the cities. Gradually, the KMT began to lose more and more ground, as they had missed their chance to eradicate the CCP and Mao in 1935. Mao began a relentless campaign, with Soviet support, to drive the KMT from several previous strongholds until Mao's triumphant march into Beijing in October of 1949. The KMT retreated to Taiwan and set up a government in exile that has existed to 2015. Recent efforts of the CCP to reconcile with Taiwan have succeeded and both countries now have a mutually beneficial relationship.

But when Mao marched into Beijing in 1949 and proclaimed the People's Republic of China on October 1, 1949, he was faced with enormous economic and social problems.

Mao Zedong announcing the founding of the People's Republic of China, Oct 1. 1949

Terms to Understand

Warlords	Marxism	Mao Zedong
KMT	Yuan Shakai	May Fourth Movement
CCP	Sun Yat-sen	1937 Japanese Invasion
Treaty of Versailles 1919	Long March	The People's Republic of China

Critical Questions:

Why did China descend into warlordism in 1912?

Why did Sun Yat-sen eventually fail to establish a Chinese Republic?

Why did Chiang Kaishek fail to establish the KMT as the government of China?

How did the Japanese incursion of 1937 affect the internal politics of China?

Why was the CCP ultimately successful in its struggle against the KMT?

Suggested Teaching Strategies

1. Handouts: Map of China
2. Creation of Teams within the Class; each team to have a CEO responsible for collecting assignments and approving the Group presentation (which should be prepared by the members of the team, not the CEO)
3. Instructor should put email address on the board for students to contact in case of emergencies or for questions before or after class. This will save both the students and the instructor time in class answering questions.
4. Instructor should clearly define the requirements of the course for the students on the board
5. Instructor should assign each individual student a Chinese company for a future presentation later in the semester.

6. Instructor should assign all students the terms and some critical questions as an in-class activity.

Chapter Two – 1949 and the Problems Faced by Mao

Handouts: Show Film: The Winter of Three Hairs (San Mao)

The Early Days of the Republic

The jubilation and euphoria of October 1, 1949 was soon replaced by long lines for rice, noodles, and other basic foodstuffs. Inflation had risen at a terrible rate and prices for common foods were outrageously high. People slept in the streets; refugees by the millions roamed the Chinese landscape. The scene was one of total chaos. The old China had failed. The new China was now here, but the Chinese people, from experience, always feared the worst.

Only 8% of the Chinese population was wealthy and successful. The other 92% were barely getting by, and a large number of them were starving as well. The situation called for immediate action, and to the credit of Mao Zedong's early years in power, he took immediate action to lessen the chaos.

He initiated price controls and squashed most of the black market operations that catered to the wealthy. He stopped inflation in its tracks through strict (some might have said overly-strict) penalties for black marketing and price violations. (In other words, if you charged an unreasonable price for rice or noodles, you were taken out and shot).

Mao made several price controls for oil, gas, and other energy items as well. Soon, after only a few months in office, a certain amount of order was restored to the cities. Mao privatized all foreign businesses and turned them into state-owned enterprises. This outraged the West, but the West was weary from fighting World War Two, and pretty much left Mao to his own devices. Mao gave equal rights to Chinese women; one of the smartest moves ever made in his time as leader of China.

Women of China would be thankful to Mao for the next 20 years, and would support him regardless of the several errors he would make in the future. Almost no issue was as important to women as equal rights.

Food lines in China in 1949

There were women and children starving in the streets of Beijing when Mao arrived in 1949. The price reforms greatly reduced the starvation problems, but there were still plenty of other problems to be solved.

Child in the streets of Beijing 1949

Millions of women and children refugees were left behind by the KMT in China. Mao and the CCP took care of the vast majority of them immediately after taking power. There were few cars in China at the time in 1949, so the energy crisis from high prices of gasoline did not affect the country as badly as it would have in modern times. Only the rich could afford cars then, anyway. Heat in the winter was a far more serious problem.

Families huddled together in cold water flats in Beijing in 1949

Initially, collective planning was used to pool food, shelter and clothing for the millions of Chinese who were lacking one or more of these life's necessities. But, as things improved in China, collectives, or communes became more and more unpopular among the Chinese. Communes were the rough equivalent of recovery programs like the WPA under the Roosevelt era in the US during the Depression.

Chinese Commune established after 1949

Communes provided basic food, shelter and clothing and little else. A few RMB a month might be saved in the more frugal families. It was an existence for survival, not an existence for prospering. Collectives soon began to go out of favor with the general population after the first few difficult years passed in the early 1950s.

The Hundred Flowers Campaign

Another social failure of the Mao regime was *The Hundred Flowers Campaign of 1956.* Mao encouraged many new opinions and suggestions for the CCP and when people began making alternate suggestions or opinions to the CCP, they were sent away to re-education camps to learn not to trust what Mao said. This cartoon perfectly illustrates the Hundred Flowers Campaign.

Censorship of Chinese Film

Previous to the 1950s, Chinese film suffered from a series of unfortunate events. Beginning in 1937, the invasion of the Japanese also brought along Japanese censorship of Chinese films in the major cities. The censorship was severe about mentioning anything negative about Japan, but otherwise mild in censoring other areas. This censorship lasted until 1945. At that time, the KMT and the CCP had intensified their civil war and few good films were made during the time period between 1945-1949. Among the better films of that era were *The Winter of Three Hairs* (San Mao) and *Spring in a Small Town*. Sadly, these would be the last two good Chinese films until the late seventies, almost thirty years in the future.

Censorship under Mao was far worse than censorship under the Japanese occupation. Every film had to have a strong socialistic message. This made love stories almost impossible. Movies about the Civil War and the Japanese were unintentionally funny. In these Red Movies, the Chinese were always brilliant and fearless, and the Japanese were always stupid and cowardly. In reality, much more of the opposite was true, or how else could have Japan conquered and ruled over half of China for over a decade? Comedies were almost non-existent, as the heavy-handed socialist content ruined any spontaneity within a humorous situation. So for thirty long years, Chinese citizens were without any legitimate Chinese cinema. This would change during the Deng years.

The Economy Under Mao in the 1950s

The Chinese economy under Mao had mixed results. Initially, his price controls to curb inflation were very good and much needed by the entire country. However, the longer that Mao was in power, the more bizarre some of his policies became. He once had a campaign to eliminate a species of a bird, for instance (which was unsuccessful). He tried to make China a leading iron-producing country, but failed to realize that China just did not have the natural resources to make that attempt.

Housing for the poor improved somewhat under Mao in the 1950s, as did the lot of Chinese women, who continued to improve their station under his tenure. Food production picked up more as a result of the ending of war and hostilities in China than because of any agricultural policies instituted by Mao. Collectives were enough to feed the burgeoning population, but not enough to make countryside farmers prosperous. Making profits and materialism were considered very bad traits under the Mao regime in the 1950s. Capitalism was usually discouraged unless it had socialistic value. Clothing of Chinese was relentlessly drab and colorless in the 1950s. The infrastructure improved slightly, as more roads were built, but the infrastructure was still behind those of developed nations. By the 1960s, China was still living like it was 1945.

Chapter Two – Terms to Understand

October 1, 1949	Chinese Women's Rights	Capitalism
State Owned Enterprises (SOEs)	Price Controls	Socialism
The Hundred Flowers Campaign	RMB	Communism
Communes	Infrastructure	Japanese Occupation

Critical Questions

1. How do SOEs differ from private companies?
2. Why do you think communes were doomed to failure?
3. Why were Mao's price controls so crucial for 1949 China?
4. How did the Japanese Occupation affect the Chinese Civil War?
5. Why were women always in the corner of Mao Zedong?

Instructor :

Show film: The Winter of Three Hairs or Spring in a Small Town

List differences between SOEs and private companies

Show the plight of Chinese women before and after Mao

Show the effects of Price Controls

Show the effects of the Japanese Occupation

Chapter Three - **Disaster in the 1960s**

The Sino-Russian Split

The Chinese economy was stagnant in the 1960s. The GNP grew by less than 2% a year and the per capita income of the average Chinese was little more than it was in 1949. Widespread starvation, for the most part, had been eliminated by Mao. During this period of 1949-1960, the CCP had maintained close ties to Stalin and the Russian Communist Party. With the ascension of Khrushchev, however, in the 1960s, China and Russia began to drift apart in their approach to nuclear weapons and foreign policy.

Khrushchev favored a confrontational approach to nuclear policy toward the United States, while Mao had been repairing fences with the West since the unsuccessful Korean War campaign. At this point in time, Russia was far more feared in the West than was China. Mao did not personally like Khrushchev, who on many occasions insulted Stalin's policies which Mao respected. This led to a worsening of China-Russian relations in the 1960s.

When border disputes between Russia and China intensified in the 1960s, the Chinese recalled all of their people in Russia, and Russia removed all of their technical and nuclear people from China. Things almost got out of hand and a nuclear exchange between the two superpowers almost took place at one point. Things got so bad that Mao ordered an underground city under Beijing to be built in case of nuclear war. A full city was built complete with many amenities, but never put into use.

Mao Begins to Fall Into Party Disfavor

By the middle of the 1960s, Mao's economic policies had placed his position of leadership in jeopardy, and he was almost overthrown by one of his most trusted generals. Mao responded with a brilliant marketing campaign using the youth of China to revitalize the country and rid himself of detractors at the same time. He did this with the assistance of his new girlfriend, Jiang Qing, a former B actress in some very bad Chinese films. The scheme that the both of them came up with would be known as The Cultural Revolution and would cost millions of Chinese their lives and livelihoods.

The major theme of the Cultural Revolution was out with the olds and in with the news; out with the olds except old Mao himself. The idea was that young people would cleanse the corruption and immobility of the CCP. On the surface, it sounded like a promising idea, but in its execution, which was filled with amazing blunders of common sense, it turned out to be one of the greatest disasters in Chinese history. The economic effects of the Cultural Revolution would also be disastrous.

At first, students were allowed free passage on Chinese trains. This caused a great loss of revenue for the train sector. After a while, the students thought they were smarter than the teachers and professors they were studying under. That was one of the first amazing blunders of this movement. The students began taking over the schools. It was like putting the inmates in charge of the insane asylum. None of the students were familiar with the day to day operations of becoming a principal or a dean of a department; they only knew that they wanted out with the old and in with the new.

The situations quickly moved from being comical to horrific. Schools were closed or used for useless sessions of Cultural Revolution rhetoric where students patted each other on the shoulder for ridding themselves of their oppressive teachers and professors. The pleas of reasonable and educated teachers and professors went on deaf ears in the Mao regime. He sided with the students. Mao knew that reason did not keep you in power, only the mob kept you in power. He was very careful never to turn the mob against himself.

The schools were now closed and used for political meetings. Children were running around wild in the streets. Parents had to quit whatever jobs they had in order to take care of children who were supposed to be in school. The young red guard took over the instruction of the primary schools as well and started teaching political thought to second and third grade children instead of reading, writing and arithmetic. This was pretty catastrophic enough, but then things took a turn for the worse.

Over the years, the Red Guard, headed by the Dragon Lady herself, Jiang Qing, recruited three other criminals to run the Cultural Revolution; they included Zhang Chunqiao, Yao WenYuan, and Wang Hongwen. It was actually the Gang of Five because Lin Biao, a leading Chinese general, was also a major figure in the conspiracy. Despite his protests, Mao himself was responsible for many of the activities of the Cultural Revolution and dictated several actions for Jiang Qing to take, but was never reprimanded by the CCP for these actions. By the time the Cultural Revolution was over, Mao was dying and the CCP figured there was little to gain by staining the name of such a prominent Chinese political figure.

Other atrocities of the Cultural Revolution occurred in the service sector. Young students ran trains, crashed them on occasions or ran them off the track. Students took over hospital administration and ordered the experienced doctors and nurses to clean the latrines while patients suffered and died from lack of proper medical care. When confronted with medical emergencies, the students became frustrated and left in a huff; leaving untreated patients to suffer and die needlessly. All of these things and much more occurred during the Cultural Revolution.

Millions of lives were disrupted when CCP officials retaliated by sending students down to communes or farms as punishment for their absence from classes. Now millions of students had to learn how to be farmers from scratch and any knowledge they may have learned from books was practically useless for that. Thousands committed suicide rather than to be "sent down" as it was called by the students and the government. Some abandoned the farms they were sent to and never seen again. Others stayed for the rest of their lives and were some of the best-educated farmers in the history of mankind.

The economic losses of the Cultural Revolution were staggering. Not only in the loss of human manhours of work and productivity, but in loss of life as well. Millions developed stress disorders and other mental problems; most of which were never treated. There was loss of productivity in practically every sector of the economy. By 1976, China had had enough of the students and the Cultural Revolution. They put the Gang of Four on trial and put them away for life. General Lin Biao disappeared on a plane heading for Russia. No one knows what happened to Lin Biao. It was speculated that he died in a plane crash in Mongolia, but there was never any body found, and he may have ended his days in the hills of Mongolia herding sheep.

Housing during this period practically came to a standstill. By 1976, there were only a few more million units than in 1949. After the death of Mao and the infusion of billions of dollars in trade balances under Deng, construction of units began rapidly increasing until it reached fever pitch just before the recession of 1998. Food prices remained fairly stable as well, never topping the 2% inflation mark from 1949 until well after the death of Mao in 1976. After food and shelter, clothing prices became the most stable of all; failing to rise over 1% in any one given year since 1949 until 2002. These are amazingly stable inflation numbers.

Despite the savings in food, shelter and clothing sectors, the Chinese economy suffered terrible losses in most other sectors during the Cultural Revolution. GDP was down, the per capita of Chinese citizens was down, positive trade balances decreased, new successful businesses were down and investments in banks and the private sector were down. Other that that, the Cultural Revolution was a real boon to China.

Terms to Understand:

The Sino-Russian Split	Khrushchev	Red Guard
GNP	Cultural Revolution	Jiang Qing
GDP	out with the olds, in with the news	Lin Biao
Per Capita Income	get sent down	Gang of Four

Critical Questions

1. How did the Sino-Russian split change Chinese foreign policy?
2. How did the Cultural Revolution begin?
3. Why was out with the olds and in with the news a bad idea?
4. How did getting sent down change one's life in China?
5. Who was the Gang of Four and what did they do?

Instructor Suggestions

Discuss the causes of the Sino-Russian Split

Discuss the causes and effects of the Cultural Revolution

Discuss the trauma of getting sent down

Chapter Four – # The Death of Mao and the Opening Up of China Under Deng

Deng Picks Up the Pieces

The mess left behind in China by Mao Zedong, Jiang Qing and the Gang of Four was of enormous proportions in 1976. The Cultural Revolution left millions displaced and other millions without family members. For ten years, the entire economic structure of China had been pummeled with Red Guard rhetoric that led to one economic disaster after another when young, inexperienced Red Guard replaced older, more experienced professionals in education, health care and other critical areas.

Deng and his family suffered like other Chinese through this period; he even got one of his sons paralyzed in a struggle session with Red Guard students. The horror would not go unpunished in the future. Deng and every Chinese leader since Mao has distrusted the motives of all student demonstrations and the memory of the Cultural Revolution, led by radical students, is always on the mind of any Chinese leader. This accounted for the harsh treatment of the Beijing University students in the Tiananmen Square incidents. There was no great outcry in China over that event, other than from college students, because the rest of China had had its fill of students trying to run the show. China will never again allow students to become too vociferous.

Deng started his rehabilitation of China with the military. The Lin Biao incident was still fresh in his mind as he drew up clear guidelines for checks and balances in the military as well as checks and balances for the Politburo and other CCP organizations. Once the military and the CCP administration was restored to order, he began to address other significant problems left behind by the Cultural Revolution.

The economy was in a shambles, there was now a thirty-year void of music, art and film creativity in China, and the educational system was shattered and needed to be reorganized almost from scratch, and the medical state of China was in a mess. It was just not one monumental task; it was several monumental tasks at the same time. In many ways, Deng Xiaoping was a greater man than Mao Zedong, because he rescued China from the catastrophe of the Cultural Revolution. Another modifying force during this time period was Zhou Enlai, who often prevented Mao from attempting even more bizarre and catastrophic policies upon China. Unfortunately, Zhou died at approximately the same time as Mao.

Deng Revamps the Medical System, Film Industry

After the military and the CCP, Deng turned his attention to the medical infrastructure of China. He immediately removed anyone who ascended to power during the Cultural Revolution. He put the most senior people in charge of every department. He required extensive experience for any doctor, hospital administrator or nurse. He gave compensation to those removed from their hospital posts during the Cultural Revolution. In essence, he fixed the medical infrastructure of China in less than one year.

A great film buff, Deng announced in his second month in power that filmmakers would now have the same creative freedoms that all the other countries in the world enjoyed. In other words , it was no longer necessary to have a strong socialist message in your film. This was an enormous relief to Chinese filmmakers, who began a flood of excellent films with the ascension of Deng to power. You could still not criticize the CCP in films, but that was a minor consideration compared to the heavy hand of Mao. Great Chinese directors such as Zhang Yimou and Chen Kaige were able to emerge with a slew of good films in the next decade.

As Chinese film came back to life, so did the social life of the Chinese. Millions started going to the movies again after decades of boredom from Red Movies and Socialist claptrap films. Theatres began popping up in every city and even in the countryside. Going to the movies was fun again. Foreign films, and in particular, US films, were now legal to show in theaters, and the Chinese flocked by the millions to see them.

Deng Tackles the Economy

Deng removed trade barriers for fast food chains to gain entry into China with much more ease than under Mao. After the great food chains like McDonalds, KFC and Hagandaaz, came the great retail chain stores like Metro from Germany and Walmart from the United States. Carefour gained entry from France. Germany started to send their quality cars to China and wealthy Chinese abandoned their inferior domestic brands of cars. Even Japan was given trade breaks to bring in their cars, electronics and motorcycles. All of these positive economic moves helped China move forward into the world of economic competition in 1980.

The infrastructure of China was in a mess. Most highways went unrepaired for almost thirty years. The train system was outdated. The airlines were consistently late and had more than their share of crashes. In short, travel between Chinese cities or to other countries was a risky undertaking. Deng laid the groundwork for the building of massive amounts of subway systems, high-speed trains and modernized highways throughout China. It would take several years, even decades, but he would succeed in most of his goals.

The rebuilding of the train system allowed people to work outside of their home towns. This increased job opportunities. Increased job opportunities led to increased Per Capita incomes among the poor, working class, and professionals as the entire Chinese population benefited from the policies of Deng. And Deng was not finished yet; not by a long shot. He intended to set up tax-free, special economic zones that were not subject to the rather strict guidelines of the CCP. This was to be his greatest of all achievements.

Meanwhile, the psyche of the Chinese population began to heal from the events of the Cultural Revolution. People moved forward with their lives. Farmers began to modestly raise the prices of their produce, small storeowners began to stock Western goods, the administration of the universities was returned to the most senior professors and administrators, and classrooms were returned to the teachers. The students were returned to their seats, where they belonged. The content of the universities and colleges was expanded to include international cooperation and several new courses and majors. Marxist thought and socialist courses were reduced, although not completely eliminated. It was a tremendous improvement in the quality of content of Chinese education.

Deng wisely retained the good things accomplished by Mao, such as providing women with equal access to colleges and universities, allowing them to vote, hold CCP office and do everything a man in China was able to do. He kept inflation and prices in check using Mao's methodology of strict control of profiteering, but with a bit less heavy hand. He initiated the beginnings of research into China entering the stock market game, and reformed banking practices to more closely mirror the banking practices of the West. One of his greatest achievements was to open China to the West and vice-versa. Now, China was once again a member of the international community.

Terms to Understand:

Deng Xiaoping	Beijing University	Walmart
Zhou Enlai	Tiananmen Square	McDonald's
Zhang Yimou	Special Economic Zone	KFC
Chen Kaige	Metro	Hagandaaz

Critical Questions

Why was Deng so important to the future of China in 1978?

Why was Zhou Enlai a calming influence on China during the Mao era?

Why were Special Economic Zones a major advance for China?

Why did the West rush in with several companies to do business in China?

Instructor Suggestions

Discuss Mao, Deng and Chinese economic reforms in the late 1970s

Discuss the Chinese film industry and it revival in the late 1970s

Discuss Tiananmen Square from all points of view

Discuss Special Economic Zones

Chapter Five – **The Special Economic Zones Boost China's Economy**

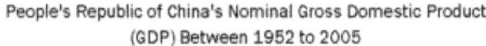
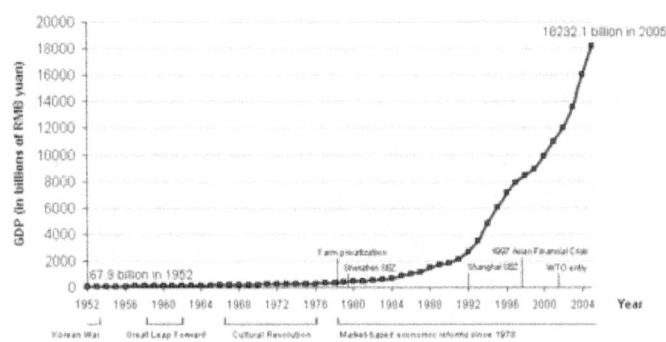

China GDP (1952-2004)

The above chart clearly shows the effect of Deng Xiaoping's policies upon the economy of China. After one or two years of cleaning up the mess left behind by Mao Zedong and the Cultural Revolution, the Chinese economy took off like a rocket with the greatest sustained percentage increase in GDP of any country in world history during a similar period.

How was Deng able make this remarkable transition? He began with *Gaige Kaifang* which translated becomes Reforms and Openness. He initiated the Four Modernizations including agriculture, industry, science and technology, and the military. He was successful in all of them except for intellectual property protection within technology. This one small omission in his policies would come back to haunt China later in the 21st century.

Even though Deng was not able to foresee the eventual problem of intellectual property protection, he nevertheless made other very significant In December of 1978, Deng announced the formal official launch of the Four Modernizations. This is considered to be the real starting point of the Reform Era. Deng was faced with a scientific community that had been isolated from the international community for almost thirty years. The university system had been isolated for the same amount of time. Equipment throughout the country was from the 1950s or even earlier.

Deng recognized the immediate need to reform all of these areas as soon as possible. Deng turned to the United Nations Development Program (UNDP) in the Fall of 1978 for assistance in getting China up to speed with the rest of the world. The introduction of the use of market principles and best business practices were a big shot in the arm for the Chinese economy.

The key advisor of the UN body was Jack Fensterstock of the United States. His efforts gained China entry into both The World Bank and Asian Development Bank resources. These provided valuable opportunities for China to rebuild itself in many different areas.

In December 1978 at the Third Plenum of the 11th Central Committee, Deng Xiaoping announced the official launch of the Four Modernizations, formally marking the beginning of the reform era. The emphasis was on strong economic self-reliance. To say the project was a success would be a great understatement.

Modernization in Agriculture

In the Modernization Strategy for agriculture, Deng implemented a number of important reforms, the most important of which was the elimination of communes and collectives. Deng believed that farmers should be given the opportunities to own their own land, raise their own crops and make their own profits. In other words, he replaced the rigid Marxist system with an open market system. This decision led to billions of additional RMB in productivity within the agriculture sector and a big boon to the Chinese economy. Getting these reforms passed through the CCP hierarchy was not easy.

Deng had to explain this reform in terms that were acceptable to the CCP. He called it the socialist market economy or socialism with Chinese characteristics. He used Lenin as an example of moving an economy forward with capitalistic policies. Deng succeeded in convincing the CCP that this would be healthy for the Chinese economy.

Deng at the Johnson Space Center in the United States

Modernization in Science and Technology

Deng was the first Chinese leader to visit the United States since Chiang Kai-Shek in the late 1940s. This round of photo-ops and softening the stance against the United States after two wars in Asia (Korean War and Vietnam War) was a big step in accelerating the economic recovery of China. Deng's foreign policy decision to distance himself and China from Russia in a similar fashion to Mao was met with approval in Washington, DC. Deng's Four Modernizations, his foreign policy decisions, and his visit to the US signaled a new beginning for China-US relations.

During Deng's visit to the US, he became enamored with the US space program and decided to enter China into the Space Race. This decision led to several technological and scientific advances within the Chinese scientific community over the next decade or so. It also led to the successful peaceful use of nuclear energy to be used for the creation of supplying part of China's enormous energy demands. Up to this point in time, China is the only major country where a nuclear disaster has not taken place at one of its plants. Safety was always the first concern of Deng in developing the nuclear sector. The US, Russia, and Japan all had major nuclear accidents in the following decades; but not China.

Non-Polluting Steam Emits from Efficient Chinese Nuclear Plant

Deng interpreted Mao with a lesser role for ideology and a greater role for market forces. His quote "socialism does not mean shared poverty" became famous among the people of China, as well as another saying of his: "it is good to be rich". Zhou Enlai was supported by Deng years earlier when Zhou advocated the new Four Modernizations. Both Zhou and Deng were the moderating forces that kept Mao from going over the deep end in the 1970's when Mao lost his credibility after the Cultural Revolution.

Modernization of the Economy

Deng made numerous reforms in the economy. He allowed municipalities and provinces to invest in industries that they considered to be the most profitable for their regions and cities. The emphasis of the Chinese economy was now export-oriented, plus the utilization of the advantage of China's least expensive labor force for light industry. These variables allowed production costs to lower for almost any product you could imagine. The low production cost of numerous items began to attract the attention of the foreign investors from the West, who wanted to lower their production costs via cheap labor. Within a short period of time, China became a hotbed of foreign investment for this purpose.

The acceleration of these investments were instigated by sound reforms in the banking system. Chinese were already notorious as the best savers of money in the world; as they often saved 50% or more of whatever salary they earned, on the average. This allowed the banks to have a heavy cash investment pool, which was also subsidized by the CCP. The more money the banks accumulated, the less dependent they became on the government. In other words, taxation became an additional income for the government, instead of subsidies draining the government budget.

This allowed the government to increase expenditures on infrastructure such as fast trains, better highways better local roads, more connections between cities and towns, more parks and recreational facilities for children, and better public housing units, as well as improved health care. The institution of the one-child policy began to curb the burgeoning Chinese population, which was now over one billion people. There were millions of exceptions to this new mandate, and countryside people were generally exempt from it. The end result was a much slower growth rate and a more manageable economy.

Special Economic Zones

After all of the four modernizations were well under way, Deng crowned his achievements with the concept of Special Economic Zones. Foreign investors were already enamored with the low production costs of goods due to inexpensive Chinese labor, and the additional lure of tax breaks and Special Economic Zones was the icing on the cake for almost every foreign investor in the world of any importance.

Deng added productivity to his list of achievements. Material and bonus incentives were begun in factories. Countryside people were now allowed to sell homegrown products. The countryside started to reduce its dependency on the cities for numerous products, and the cities benefited from the lower prices for produce from surplus crops. In short, both the countryside and the cities prospered. Under the KMT, only the cities prospered, under Mao, no one prospered during the Cultural Revolution, and now everyone had a piece of the pie.

Deng's Farewell Tour of SEZs

Deng made a farewell tour in the Spring of 1992. He visited Guangzhou, Shenzhen, Zhuhai, Shanghai, and Xiamen in order to reassert his economic agenda. He continued to champion the opening up of China and economic reform. The tour solidified Deng's hold on the CCP, with Jiang Zemin submitting to the wishes of Deng for the tour to be publicized. One area of weakness in Deng's arguments, however, was that " some areas must get rich before others". This did not go over well in Beijing or the Central and Western parts of China. Deng died in 1997 and Jiang Zemin would continue his policies well into the 21st century. The UN, France, Britain, Canada, and especially the United States gave Deng several honors.

Terms to Understand:

GDP	World Bank	Inexpensive Labor
Gaige Kaifang	**Asian Development Bank**	**Foreign Investment**
Four Modernizations	Johnson Space Center	One Country, Two Systems
UNDP	Low Productions Costs	Jiang Zemin

Critical Questions:

1. How did China's GDP react to Deng's Reforms?
2. How did the Four Modernizations aid economic reforms?
3. How did the UNDP aid China's economic reforms?
4. Why were low production costs and inexpensive labor closely connected in China?
5. Why did Special Economic Zones attract enormous foreign investment?

Instructor:

Discuss Gaige Kaifang

Discuss the Four Modernizations

Discuss the importance of low production costs and inexpensive labor

Discuss foreign investment based on SEZ benefits

Chapter Six – The Chinese Economy Eventually Prospers Under Jiang Zemin (1989-2002)

Jiang Zemin became prominent during the Tiananmen Square protests. Zhao Ziyang, the previous Party Secretary, had been deemed too tolerant of the student protesters in Beijing by Deng. Deng removed Zhao and Jiang became the compromise candidate to replace him. Previously, Jiang had been the Mayor of Shanghai, and had shown a firm hand in shutting down an overzealous Shanghai newspaper that was critical of the CCP.

After a tentative start to his regime, Jiang backed Deng during his Southern China Economic Tour and sped up his economic reforms to conform with the expectations of Deng. It is safe to say that the first half of Jiang's tenure was beset by numerous domestic problems which adversely affected his ability to match Deng's previous successes. Migration to cities was becoming unchecked, crime rates rose dramatically in the cities, unemployment rose as a result of the closing of several State-Owned Enterprises (SOEs) that were unable to employ the newly displaced workforce. Corruption was at an all-time high, and went virtually unchecked.

Jiang successfully rose up to the challenge of the Falun Gong, a powerful cult with millions of followers in China and throughout the world. His no-nonsense repression of this group met with the general approval of the Chinese populace and his stock rose in political circles. Jiang pursued strong international trade as a continuing impetus to the Chinese economy. He had cordial relations with Clinton and both leaders exchanged visits. From 1997 onwards, China maintained an average of 8% or higher GDP growth for several years until 2002. This figure was unmatched by any other major country in the world during this period.

Under Jiang, Hong Kong was returned to China by the United Kingdom and Macao was returned to China by Portugal. These were two major accomplishments for any Chinese leader. Jiang was also able to get China into the World Trade Organization and positioned China for a successful bid to host the 2008 Olympics. These two additional coups resulted in billions of dollars of investment in China's infrastructure and economic institutions.

Jiang made a concentrated effort to trade successfully with both Russia and the United States without favoring either major power. This was not an easy balancing act. It became known as balancing the Bear and the Eagle. Also during his tenure, Jiang made substantial inroads into investing into trade with Africa. He deduced that he could trade building African infrastructure in exchange for several billion tons of African raw materials at extremely low wholesales prices. China, in effect, succeeded, where several European countries had failed in Africa in the previous century. The Jiang African Strategy is still in force in modern China. He did it by not interfering with local African politics, but just by trading infrastructure for raw materials. None of the other European countries had figured that simple solution out.

Jiang pictured above with Bill Clinton

Weaknesses of the Jiang regime appeared to be a benign neglect of the Chinese environmental problems at the cost of economic development. In addition, widespread corruption became commonplace and threatened to undermine the continuing prosperity of the economy. To that end, party leaders focused on a successor to Jiang who would address both of those key issues as a reform candidtate. That candidate turned out to be Hu Jintao.

Terms to Understand:

Zhao Ziyang	Return of Hong Kong	Jiang African Strategy
Countryside Migration	Return of Macao	Hu Jintao
Widespread Corruption	Falun Gong	Environmental Problems
Beijing Olympics 2008	Balancing the Bear and Eagle	Reform Candidate

Critical Questions:

Why was Zhao Ziyang removed as Party Secretary?

Why would countryside migration to the cities become an enormous problem if unchecked?

How could widespread corruption undermine a successful economy?

Why were the return of Hong Kong and Macao important to the economy of mainland China?

How did Jiang's African Strategy work?

Instructor Suggestions

Discuss the aftermath of the Tiananmen Incident in political and economic terms.

Discuss how widespread corruption can undermine an economy.

Discuss how environmental problems can be very costly to an economy

Discuss Jiang's African Strategy.

Chapter Six – The Chinese Economy Overheats and the Migration Problem Becomes More Serious

One of the leading indicators of any country's economy is the state of its real estate market. By 2002, the state of China's real estate market, which primarily consisted of apartments built in its major cities, was beginning to overheat. Overheating meant that inflated prices were being paid for simple three and four room apartments that were far over the fair market value of the properties. There were several factors that contributed to this situation.

One factor was the ability of a buyer to not need more than 10% of the purchase price of the apartment in order to obtain a bank loan for the balance. This was quite similar to the practice of stockbrokers in 1929 in the United States who allowed buyers to buy 100% of a stock purchase with only putting down 10% of the money. This was called buying on margin. When the stock market collapsed in 1929, the United States discontinued this unsound banking practice, but it seems as if China had never studied this part of US history.

Chinese citizens are continuing to buy these apartments as an investment on margin with the hope that they will continue to rise in price in the future. This is just as dangerous as the practices of 1929 stock purchasers. Unlike 1929, however, the Chinese government has many more billions of dollars in reserve to bail out any unfortunate buyers. Regardless of the bailouts, it still remains a very dangerous economic game to play and a very expensive proposition for the government to bail out investors when the bubble finally bursts at some point in the future.

Some apartments in Beijing sell for over ten million RMB. This is the equivalent of over one and a half million US dollars. In the US, you can buy a very nice four bedroom house with every possible amenity, have a two-car garage, and a large tract of private lane and still have enough left over to buy two luxury cars to put in that garage. And you would STILL have money left over. In Beijing, all you get is the apartment. Which would you rather have?

Even in the lesser cities of China, apartments sell for in excess of one million RMB, or almost two hundred thousand dollars US. There are practically no apartments in the US that sell for that amount of money, unless they are located in the center of a major city or are located right next to the ocean. It appears as if the US real estate market offers far more value than the China real estate market.

The CCP has been trying to cope with this problem for over a decade; limiting the purchase of the apartments to people who are actually living in them, rather than those speculating and buying to resell. But it is practically impossible for authorities to determine who will actually live in the apartments and who is actually just buying them for investments. Real estate professionals only care if the buyer has the necessary down payment; they really do not care about the government's concerns about second and third apartments for investors.

Expensive Beijing Apartments: 10,000,000 RMB

This leads to some very interesting possible scenarios. When the bubble does burst, what will be the effect? The real estate developers will get their money; so they are safe, but the buyers will be stuck with properties that may fall by as much as 50% or more depending on the selling panic; and there will be a selling panic at some point in the future. The market is fine when people are buying, but if the market values of these properties start to decline, you can bet there will be a line forming in the morning of owners trying to sell their properties below the prices they paid for them.

When the fall finally takes place, there will be a domino effect throughout the economy. Many people will still owe 90% of the loan they have taken out to buy the property in the first place; just like 1929. It will make no economic sense for them to pay the mortgage loan, so they will just give the properties back to the bank and take the loss of the down payment; the banks will become owners of thousands of apartments that are now poisoned assets. If a bank has enough of these poisoned assets, they will go under as well. The government will be forced to support the banks to prevent them from going out of business. This will require billions of dollars.

Those billions of dollars will come out of a fixed budget that has a fixed number in a pie of 100%. In other words, the bailout will suck out X % of the budget from all the other lines in the national Chinese budget, such as National Defense, Education, Health Care, Social Security and infrastructure. This will have an immediate effect of slowing down the economy (which actually might be a good thing; but not if it is too drastic a slowdown). Fewer infrastructure projects will be launched; fewer hospitals will be built, more manhours will be lost to sickness and disability resulting from medical inefficiency, businesses will have a reduction in sales, restaurants will have fewer customers, and fewer luxury items will be purchased. Jobs will be cut, and unemployment will increase noticeably. All these and many other negative economic reactions will take place. Hopefully, China will avoid this draconian scenario, but not if they do not stop 1929 practices.

Another major problem affecting the current Chinese economy for over a decade is the migration problem. The great disparity between countryside and city per capita income has forced millions of countryside workers to involuntarily migrate to cities. Sometimes these cities are a thousand miles away from their home towns. The migrants come to the cities by the millions and it creates a whole series of problems for China's economy.

Chinese countryside migrant workers living in the shadow of million RMB apartment houses

First and foremost, the very place the Chinese government is trying to build up, the countryside, is losing its best minds and most qualified people to the cities. What is left behind is usually women, children and old men plus a few uneducated, unemployable men who are only qualified for farming duties. Some of the women are quite capable of handling administrative and professional duties for the country's building up of the countryside, but there are usually not enough of them to do the job properly. This means that the government has to send an army of officials to outlying areas. These are generally people who do not want to be there in the first place; and many of which do not have anything in common with the natives who live there. This situation causes a whole new set of problems.

Another very serious problem from this mass migration is the overloading of city low-cost apartments. There is already an underclass in each Chinese city. These people are constantly looking for low-cost housing. The additional competition of migrant workers coming to their city adds to the difficulty of finding suitable housing at a reasonable cost. Migrant workers, as a result, also have a more difficult time finding suitable housing at a reasonable cost. Both groups will now live in more substandard apartments that cost more money a month.

Chinese countryside migrant worker children

A factor overlooked by many government officials is health care. The migrants who flock to the cities have scant resources for health care. Consequently, when they get sick, they have a tendency to spread their diseases to other natives of the cities they have migrated to. The additional burden of migrant workers strains the emergency rooms and regular hospital services that are offered in most cities. Budgets and working hours are increased for hospital workers at the cost of other important budget lines for hospital and other city services. Consequently, everyone in the city gets less individual quality care.

Some migrants bring their wives; others bring their entire family of children and wives. Of course, the migrants who bring wives and children create a whole new array of problems for themselves and the cities they migrate to. Now, in addition to health care problems, the family will be faced with the schooling problems of their children. Millions of migrants cannot afford city schools for their children and opt to just leave them at home with their wives. It is very difficult to save any significant amount of money for migrant workers who bring their family members with them to the cities.

The places where migrant workers tend to live in cities is usually the place in the city with the highest rate of crime. Although the nature of the crime is usually petty theft, it can dramatically affect the lives of the migrant workers who have moved there. Even a minor petty theft from a migrant worker family can have a huge impact and how much money that family saves that year. Almost none of these petty crimes are reported to the local police because migrant workers and their families tend to keep a very low profile in the cities in which they work.

Children Left Behind by Migrant Workers in Countryside School

Education of migrant workers for new skills as well as education for any members of the migrant worker's family is practically zero. There is not enough time in the day for migrant workers to become re-educated in other areas; they are too busy working 16 hours a day in order to save money for their families. Education for their wives and children is usually not an alternative; anything that costs extra money is usually not an alternative. The government might benefit by establishing programs in these cities to educate the families of migrant workers for free. This, in turn, might allow the migrant workers and their families to return to their home towns in a more efficient manner, thus solving two problems in one stroke.

Terms to Understand:

Buying on Margin	Migrant Education	Countryside Per Capita Inequity
Bailouts	Health Care Overload	Education Overload
Migrant Housing	Housing Shortage	Countryside Abandonment
Migrant Health Care	Countryside Shortages	Apartment Inflation

Critical Questions

Why is buying apartments in Beijing on margin a dangerous economic practice?

Why will the government eventually have to bail out banks in Beijing for this practice?

Why are migrants workers such a serious problem for China?

How do migrant workers adversely affect the Chinese economy?

How are social services strained by migrant workers?

Instructor Suggestions

Discuss the dangers of buying apartments in large Chinese cities.

Discuss possible future scenarios of real estate markets that finally go bust.

Discuss the problems of migrant workers in China.

Discuss the problems for the government concerning migrant workers in China

Chapter Seven - The Problem of IPP (Intellectual Property Protection)

One of the greatest economic problems of the Chinese government in the last decade is the problem of IPP (Intellectual Property Protection). I will be the first to tell you that I enjoy downloading all the free music, movies and software that is available on the Chinese internet. So do hundreds of millions of Chinese. Everything is free! What could be bad about that? How can it possibly adversely affect the Chinese economy?

There is a person or a group of people behind the creation of software. This person wants to be paid a reasonable amount of money for the materials they have created. In China, this person's material will be all over the internet for free within a matter of minutes after the material has been created and published in China. This results in greatly reduced income for the creator of this software and is unacceptable from the view of the software creator. Two things immediately occur after events like these.

Chinese software developers are leaving China in Droves because of IPP

The better minds of tech within the Chinese population are not stupid. They know when their software is not creating the revenue streams that it is supposed to create. If creating software in China does not meet their expectations for revenue creation, then the software developers will create their software in more secure environments in surrounding countries in Asia that have strict IPP controls, such as Japan, Australia and Singapore. Millions of tech people leave China and resettle in countries like the United States, Canada, or Germany. Most of them never return to China to live but come to visit relatives and friends. They are gone forever as intellectual assets of the Chinese economy.

The cost to the Chinese economy of the loss of these millions of talented tech workers is in the billions of US dollars. Continued loss via a brain drain to the Chinese economy is really not an option for China. Since China still trails in tech badly to countries in Asia like India and Japan, it is essential that China retain these talented people within their country. If China fails to take draconian steps to improve IPP within China, it will pay for the lack of IPP in the future with billions of lost dollars in the tech sector. I really don't think the luxury of free movies, music and software is worth destroying the tech sector of the Chinese economy.

The problem of IPP in music and movies is not quite as serious (unless you are in the movie or music business). Producers of music and movies in China still make substantial profits despite illegal downloads of their products. Artists make less money, but they will make much less money if they move to another country, as Chinese music and film is not appreciated as much in other countries as it is in China. So they cannot take the same road as the software developers.

If the Chinese government does take steps to dramatically increase IPP, they will have to make a complete makeover of the Chinese internet. Companies or web sites will no longer be able to offer free music, movies or software of any type without the expressed consent of the creators of that music, movie or software. No shareware, free movie sites, free music sites, or free software sites will be allowed. Penalties should be severe enough for violators to get the message quickly and painfully. I am sure these changes will be painful for millions of Chinese who have become accustomed to free music, movies and software. I will have to pay for these things when I go back to the US in 2016, so I guess they will be paying at some point in the future as well; one way or the other.

Terms to Understand:

IPP	Brain Drain	Chinese Internet
Chinese IPP	Free Music, Movies and Software	Shareware
US IPP	IPP Damage to the Economy	IPP Penalties
Software Developer	Singapore IPP	IPP Benefits

Critical Questions

How can free music, movies and software be bad?

Why is Chinese IPP very weak?

Why is US IPP very strong?

Why do software developers in China leave China for good?

Chapter Nine – The Bullet Train and the Three Gorges Project

Over the last few decades, a few of the accomplishments within the Chinese infrastructure that have significantly aided China's economy are the bullet train and the Three Gorges Project. Both of these projects ran into the billions of dollars from planning to implementation stage. Both projects had several difficult problems to overcome and both were eventually successful in creating billions of dollars to add to China's already healthy economy.

Before the bullet train, China was dependent on slow, but dependable trains that connected all the major, and several minor cities within China. But there were limitations to these trains. For example, the average speed was less than fifty miles per hour. This meant a trip from Tianjin to Beijing, which is approximately 200 miles, would take you over four hours. This was ok if you were going to travel to Beijing for the weekend, or a longer stay, but was not practical for someone who lived in Tianjin to work in Beijing.

The bullet train has increased Chinese Trade

The bullet train changed all of that and more. Now, a citizen who lived in Tianjin could reach Beijing in less than one hour. Now you could live in Tianjin and work in Beijing. This same situation occurred in over 500 cities in China at the same time. Now people in over 500 cities could live in one city and work in another. This led to tremendous opportunities for people in several cities that they never had before.

It increased economic opportunity. That increased per capita income, which, in turn, increased national GDP. People displaced by the bullet train received substantial compensation.

The bullet train has allowed migrant workers to get back to their home towns more frequently. This has reduced one part of the migrant worker problem, but there is still much for the Chinese government to do in that area. Migrant workers can now have their families visit them in the big cities and then return back to the hometowns in a timely manner, instead of taking twenty hour bus rides that are both uncomfortable and dangerous.

The bullet train has increased trade between major cities. The more people who ride the trains from one city to another, the greater the business intercourse that takes place in both of the cities. All cities that are connected to the bullet train system prosper more as a result of high-speed train service. The United States could learn from China in this respect.

There were some problems, of course, in the building of the bullet train. The train primarily travels in a straight line, so that any land that is on either side of the bullet train must become Eminent domain. This affected several cities, hundreds of small towns, and some rural areas as well. The end effect was that people were displaced from entire sections of cities, entire towns were emptied, and a few rural areas were confiscated. These were unfortunate, but necessary byproducts of the bullet train system. Putting through this kind of system in the United States would be much more controversial and difficult. The media would be full of sad stories of forced resettlement. These stories were kept to a minimum in China.

However, it is a bit eerie, when taking a bullet train ride in China, to see several small towns completely deserted, just like the old ghost towns of the Old West in the United States. Rows of completely deserted apartment houses, stores and farmhouses; all completely empty. Some towns seemed to have recovered from the process, however; they have active town activity all the way up the bullet train station. The same process would probably take place in the US, if it ever undertook such a difficult endeavor.

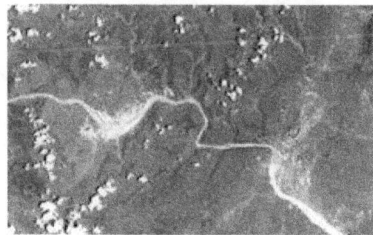

Three Gorges Project create more economic opportunity

The other great accomplishment of the Chinese that has led to greater economic prosperity was the completion of the Three Gorges Project. This project also had major difficulties that had to be overcome before its completion. Millions of Chinese were dispossessed of their riverside residences and businesses. Land that was previously available by the rivers suddenly became completely covered by water. Farmers lost their farms, businesses lost their prosperous river businesses, and residents whose families went back thousands of years lost their houses and apartments. All citizens displaced by the project were substantially compensated.

Though a heavy price was paid for this project to be completed, the economic results are uncontestable. The project provided badly needed energy via electricity throughout the area covered by the Three Gorges. The project was similar to the US TVA, or Tennessee Valley Authority, which dispossessed several thousand US citizens in the 1930s in order to build a much needed TVA for energy and water conservation. Flooding in the area of the Three Gorges has been reduced dramatically, and thousands of lives that were normally lost in flooding over the years are now being saved from that fate due to the stable construction of the project.

Chinese ghost city; caused by a major project

One social problem that arose from both projects was Social Displacement. Displacement is a normal resettling in another area of the town or city and was done without too much difficulty for the majority of the displaced. But in some cases, citizens were forced to move to another city entirely, or another town entirely. This led to Social Displacement, which means you do not have the same status socially that you had in your previous neighborhood. You must now re-establish yourself in the pecking order within your new town or city. Some displaced persons found this to be a monumental task. But the greater good seems to have been served by Eminent Domain.

Terms to Understand:

Eminent Domain	water conservation	compensation
Resettlement	energy production	displacement
Flood control	Three Gorges Project	Social displacement
TVA	ghost towns	Greater Good

Critical Questions

Why is Eminent Domain necessary?

Why was the bullet train an economic success?

Why was the Three Gorges Project an economic success?

How were common citizens adversely affected by both projects?

Instructor Suggestions

Discuss Eminent Domain

Discuss the bullet train

Discuss the Three Gorges Project

Discuss the effects of these projects on common Chinese citizens

Chapter Ten - **The Hu Jintao Era (2002-2012)**

Former Chinese leader, Hu Jintao

In general, Hu Jintao's tenure as leader of China would have to be classified as economically successful. Hu was responsible for considerable investments in both Africa and South America which paid off handsomely in economic terms. In general, Hu and China offered infrastructure improvements in the billions to each continent in return for billions of dollars of raw materials that China needed for its domestic expansion of infrastructure. The excess of these materials were sold on the open market for a substantial profit.

Hu always had a deep mistrust of the educational leaders in Beijing and all college students in general. This was due to his father being sent down during the Cultural Revolution by factions controlled by Red Guards, mostly recruited from that precise sector, Beijing college students. No Chinese leader since Deng Xiaoping has ever let the college students in China dictate or change any agenda developed by the CCP. The new leader, Xi Jinping, is now continuing that policy. Hu concentrated on maintaining China's furious economic growth during his tenure, and was successful in the vast majority of instances. While not trusting Chinese college students, Hu generally used more tact in dealing with them than did his predecessors. Hu supported Deng in the Tiananmen Incident, and his stock went up in the CCP.

Hu avoided the problems of the Global Financial Crisis by changing the emphasis of China's import and export trade to focus more on domestic consumption, rather than foreign markets. This allowed China to insulate itself during the financial crisis. One of the weaknesses of Hu's tenure was the inability of the government to confront and eliminate large cliques of corruption within the Chinese government. This drawback was one of the main reasons for the eventual emergence of Xi Jinping, a virulent anti-corruption candidate.

Xi Jinping: Current Secretary General and leader of China in 2015

Xi Jinping has successfully carried out the continued economic success of China since Hu Jintao stepped down in 2012. His policy of anti-corruption has been partially successful, but thousands of corrupt officials throughout China still remain. Corruption within the CCP is still a major problem within the country.

One of the unfortunate side-effects of a one-party system like the CCP is the potential for selling party favors for money. The two-party systems of most Western countries has some of this problem as well, but to a much lesser extent because of the checks and balances in place among the three branches of government in most democracies. The two-party system is also good for keeping corruption to a minimum because no one will watch you closer than your hated opponents.

Because there are no effective opponents to the CCP, a vast number of CCP officials run unopposed in elections and begin to accrue abnormal amounts of money and power. This leads directly to the massive corruption problem. The success of the Chinese economy has put the corruption problem on the back burner for the last forty years in China, but Xi is trying to make it a central issue. Whether he will be successful, or only partly successful in the future remains to be seen.

Part Two: The Current State of Affairs in China and Economic Case Studies

Chapter Eleven – The Current State of Affairs in China

Here is a current (2015) SWOT (strengths, weaknesses, opportunities and threats) analysis of China:

Strengths

1. **Only 8% of GDP is spent on National Defense** – China generally minds its own business in Asia and the rest of the world. Negotiations with other countries generally revolve around economic issues such as natural resources in exchange for infrastructure and other specialties of China. Military protection is almost never discussed in foreign relations and is primarily considered a domestic issue. The low percentage of the GDP that is spent on National Defense allows China to redistribute several billions of dollars into other critical areas of the budget within China. This gives China a distinct economic advantage over the United States and other Western countries that have inflated National Defense budgets (i.e. Russia, Pakistan).
2. **Homoginized Society** – Although China has numerous minorities, the vast majority of Chinese are of Han origin (90%+). This allows for shared economic, philosophical and political belief systems. The belief system of Confucianism is firmly planted within the Han culture of China. A secondary shared belief system is elements of philosophical (and sometimes superstitious elements) of Taoism. This has contributed to the relatively progressive and peaceful society China has experience over the last forty years.
3. **Infrastructure** – Although weak in the area of primary and secondary roads, China excels in the rapid transportation of its citizens through its Bullet Train system; something not possessed by most Western countries, and, in particular, a weakness of the United States. This valuable asset allows Chinese citizens to live in one city and work in another without taking cars to work. In addition to being environmentally sound, it also provides a major boost to the Chinese economy by increasing job opportunities for its citizens; another weakness of the United States economic system, which is still dependent on the car system, which travels at less than a quarter of the speed of the Bullet Train system.
4. **Population – (also a Weakness)** – The population of China is a major strength because it allows for the lowest labor costs in the world. This, in turn, allows for the lowest production costs in the world, which explains why the vast majority of companies in the world have factories in

China, or operate at an economic disadvantage. Generally speaking, the Chinese have the lowest prices for most goods and services in the world. Their food, shelter, clothing and transportation costs are the lowest in the world and dwarf the savings of countries like the United States and other Western democracies.

5. **The One-Party System (also a Weakness)** – The major strength of the one-party system is that is gets things done; and it gets them done much faster than Western countries with two-party systems. Projects like the Bullet Train and the Three Gorges Project would take far longer to complete (and some are never even started) in Western Countries because of political infighting between the two parties. In the United States and other Western countries, politics takes precedence over cooperation.
6. **The Economy** – the Chinese economy has been strong for almost forty years in succession; an unprecedented occurrence in any country in the modern era of man. This has allowed the average Chinese citizen to have several economic opportunities that their Western counterparts do not have in less active economies like the United States. There is always a job available in China if you want one. Unfortunately, several Western countries, including the United States, cannot make that claim.

Weaknesses

1. **Corruption (The One Party System)** – The number one weakness of China is corruption, which is directly traceable to the one party system of the CCP. Xi Jinping and the rest of the CCP are trying to address this serious problem, but have only been met with limited success so far, because the problem is so entrenched in current Chinese society (actually China has thousands of years of tradition in corruption due to previous one-party systems such as dynasties). This problem causes billions of lost GDP.
2. **Population** – The one-child system was successful for a period of time, but now restrictions have become so lax than any Chinese can have as many children as they want. The overpopulation of China has been a problem for China for centuries, and will not be solved anytime soon. Overpopulation causes severe strains on infrastructure, food, shelter, medical services and other critical services within China. Laws and law enforcement are almost impossible to implement when populations rise to the levels existing in China.
3. **Countryside Migration** – Millions of Chinese are migrating from the countryside to the cities to try and increase their yearly incomes. This is putting a tremendous strain on China's basic services for cities; including food supply, shelter and housing, medical services and education; all of which are becoming watered down to provide services for everyone. The strains on city budgets are also critical.
4. **Environmental Problems** – China is degrading in several areas of the environment. Pollution control is almost non-existent because of the population problem and budget restraints due to countryside migration and other issues. Pollution and land degrading is still occurring at dangerous levels and has already impacted the health care sector.

5. **Brain Drain** – China suffers from a severe shortage of tech experts because of illegal downloading of music, film and software on the Chinese internet. Once a professional tech person creates a software program in China, it appears for free on the Chinese internet in a matter of days. This has caused mass migration of the tech sector to other countries that have strong IPP (Intellectual Property Protection) laws on the books and which are enforced. Some of these professionals return to China; but most do not.
6. **Infrastructure Problems** – China has several major travel arteries that are in disrepair. Almost all of the secondary roads have some type of problem as well. Cars are not an optimum form of travel in most of China. Trains, motorcycles, and bikes are much preferred by the vast majority of the population. This leads to two lane highways on most sidewalks on both sides of a typical Chinese street. Motorcycles and bikes constantly restrict sidewalk travel of pedestrians.

Opportunities

1. **Economic Supremacy in Asia** – China will soon be replacing Japan as the number one economic force in Asia. Although trailing Japan in car production, motorcycle production, electronics and tech, it has surpassed its hated opponent because of its low production costs for every product under the sun. The factories of the world are in China; this has led to its economic supremacy in Asia. With reforms in government and continued sensible international trade policies, China can keep its number one position for many years in the foreseeable future.
2. **Increased Economic Influence in the World** – For the same exact reasons China has emerged as the leading power in Asia, so it will emerge as one of the leading economic powers in the world as well; it is only a matter of time. China must address it's corruption, migration, brain drain, environmental issues, and infrastructure problems, however, to begin challenging the big Western powers.
3. **International Political Influence** – Because China primarily negotiates its treaties based on economics rather than military considerations, it has increased its political stock in continents such as Africa and South America, while the West, and particularly the United States, has lost market share in both of those continents to China. China does not meddle in the internal affairs of other countries; a major weakness of the United States and other Western countries. As a result, when China speaks in the UN, there are several sympathetic listeners.
4. **Migration of Bullet Train Technology** – Although lacking in several other areas of tech, China excels in rapid train technology. China is the leading rapid-train developer in the world. This gives them tremendous first to market opportunities in almost every country in the world for which they can trade for precious natural resources or other valuable commodities.
5. **Increased Presence in the China Sea** – China has an extensive underutilized coastline. The development of the Chinese Navy and of the Chinese commercial nautical services could provide an additional asset to the already thriving Chinese economy. This will eventually pose problems to Western countries operating in Asia, as China begins to bite into the Western market share for shipping and other nautical assets.

6. **Peaceful Co-existence With Muslim Countries** – China currently enjoys relatively peaceful co-existence with Muslim countries for two primary reasons. First, China has a much larger Muslim population in its outlying regions than do any Western countries, and secondly, and probably more importantly, China never interferes in the internal affairs of Muslim countries (i.e. Iraq, Afghanistan etc). This policy serves China well in economic exchanges with Muslim countries.

THREATS

1. **The Environment** – The Chinese juggernaut may come to a halt internally rather than from some external force. The environmental problems of China have now reached critical levels that will adversely affect their economy by billions of US dollars, unless drastic actions are taken in the near future. The health costs alone will be in the trillions.
2. **Japan** – Japan has been a threat to China for over a hundred years. It continues to threaten China in the China Sea, the Daiyou Islands, with military buildup, with its inability to compensate China for World War Two actions, with its lack of apologies for World War Two atrocities committed against China, and because it dominates tech, cars, motorcycles, and electronics in the Asian theater. Japan is also the number one economic opponent of China.
3. **Russian Instability** – The economic instability of Russia, which shares an enormous border with China, can adversely affect the Chinese economy. A disruption in gas distribution or some other calamity within Russia can cause a great deal of damage to the Chinese energy system.
4. **US Military Presence** – United States traditional military presence in Australia, Taiwan, Japan, the Philippines, and other areas in Asia is abrasive to Chinese sensibilities. The US would not like China to be within a few hundred miles of its borders in Cuba, Mexico, Canada, or Latin America, so why would China be happy with a US presence within a few hundred miles of its borders?
5. **India** – India is a major threat to Chinese economic domination in Asia. India has a population that closely follows the Chinese in numbers, but is wracked by the Hindi-Muslim split; something not as critical in China. India does have two advantages that China does not have; its mastery of English (the international language of money) and its massive tech sector, which dwarfs the Chinese tech sector. This is due to greater IPP in India. If trends continue, China will eventually become dependent on India for tech. Not a good result for the Chinese economy.
6. **Internal Problems** – One of the biggest threats to China is China itself. The corruption, pollution, migration problems, brain drain, and infrastructure problems, if not checked and contained, can spiral out of control and cause enormous damage to the prosperous Chinese economy.

Terms to Understand:

One-Party System	Environmental Threats	Japanese Threat
Two-Party System	Russian Economic Instability	Bullet Train Technology
Global Financial Crisis	Muslim Countries	Indian Threat
SWOT	Non-Interference Policy	US Military Presence

Critical Questions

How is the One-Party system an advantage for China?

How is the One-Party system a disadvantage for China?

Why is a SWOT analysis of China important?

How can the environment destroy an economy?

Why do the Chinese consider Japan a threat?

Instructor Suggestions

Discuss China-Japan relations

Discuss one and two party systems

Discuss a SWOT analysis of China

Discuss the importance of the Chinese environment

Chapter Twelve – **Case Studies of Major Chinese Companies**

Agricultural Bank of China

Sales

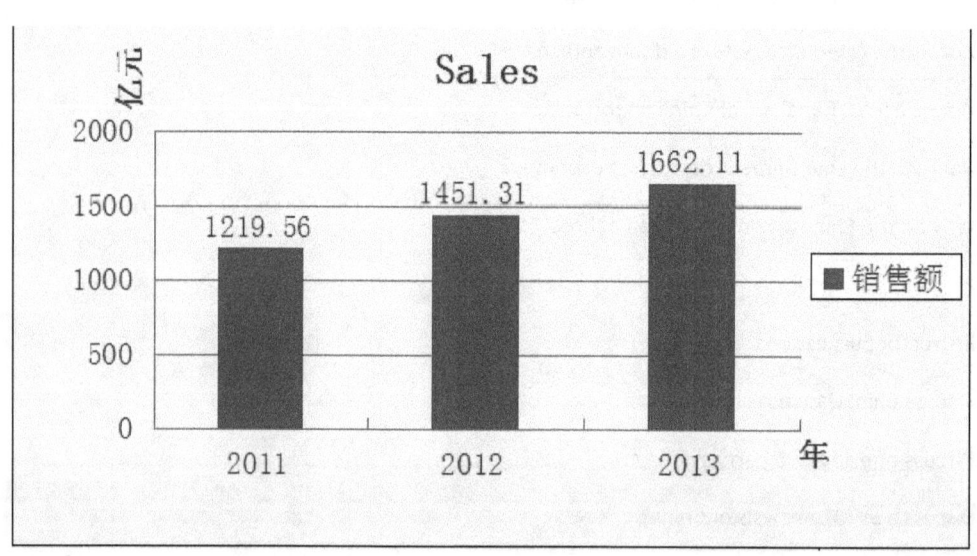

Domestic Sales = 3 points

International Sales = 0 points

Total Sales Score = 3 points

Market Share

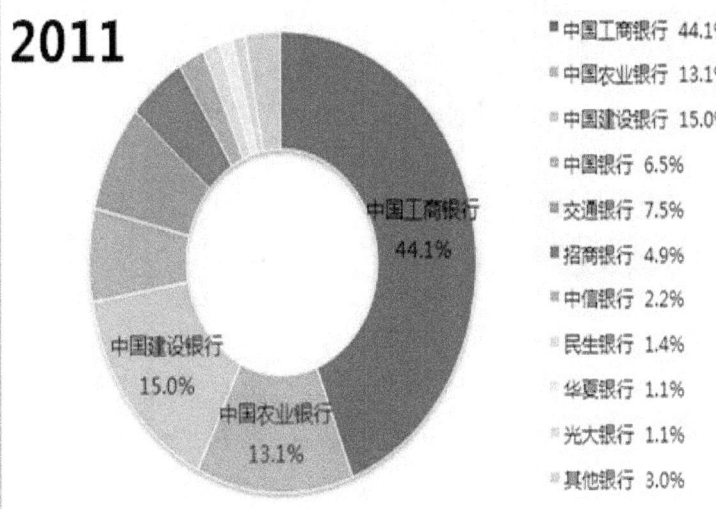

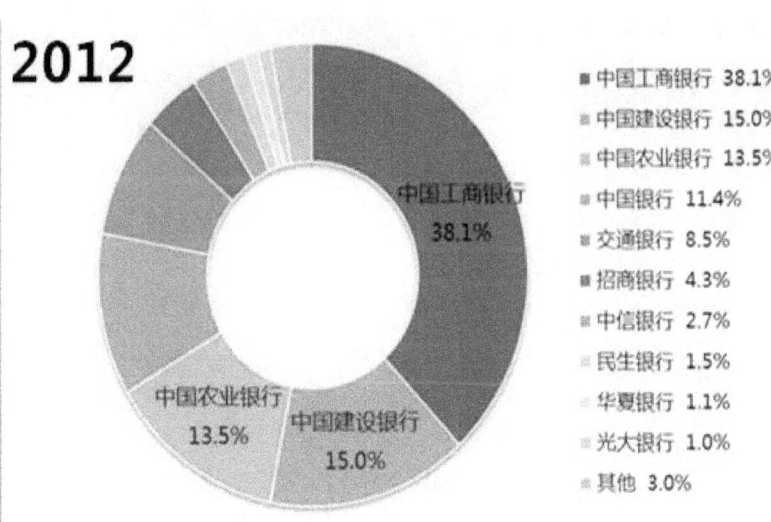

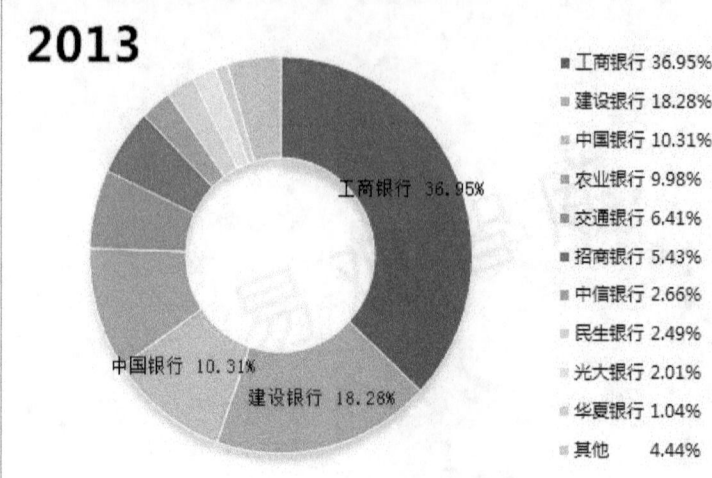

Domestic Market Share Score = 1 pt (market share down in 2013 = -2)

International Market Share Score = 0 pts

Total Market Share Score = 1 pt

Stock Price

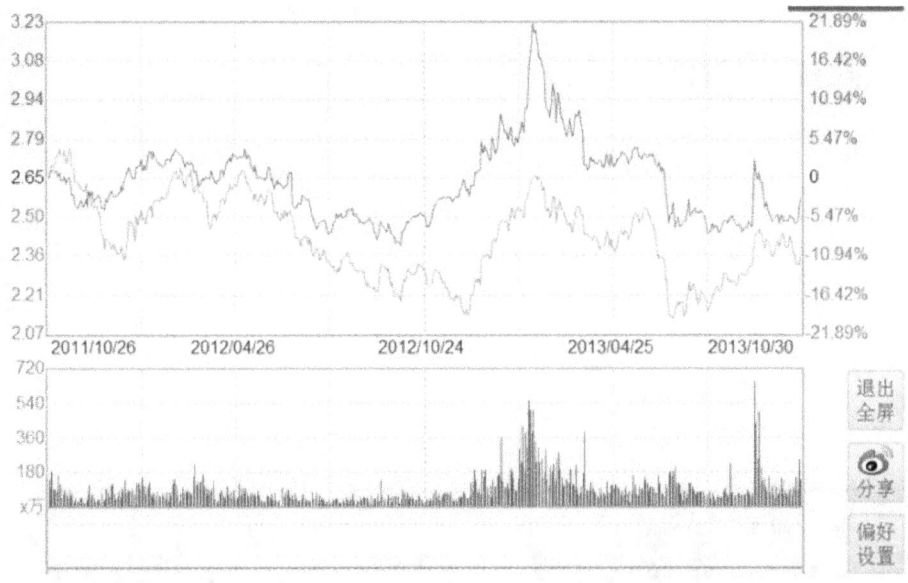

Stock Price = 1 point increase in 2012; -2 points for decrease in 2013

Volatility = 2 points for three year period; -2 points for volatility in 2013

Total Score for Stock Price = -1 point

Total Score All Sections = 4 points = 20%

Rating - Unacceptable; poor market share and stock perfomance

Air China

Sales 销售额	2011	2012	2013
	1219.56	1451.31	1662.1

单位：亿元   SALES

1800

Domestic Sales = 3 points

International Sales = 3 points

Total Sales Points = 6 points

Market Share - 2011

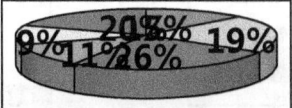

- air china
- sourthern airlines
- Eastern airlines
- United airlines
- Xiamen airlines
- other

market share – 2012

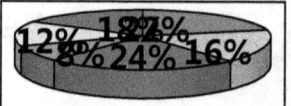

- air china
- sourthern airlines
- Eastern airline
- United airlines
- Xiamen airlines
- other

market share - 2013

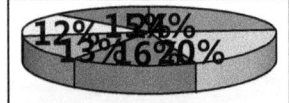 

Domestic Score = 3 points

International Score = 3 points

Total Score Market Share = 6 points

Stock Price

2011

2012

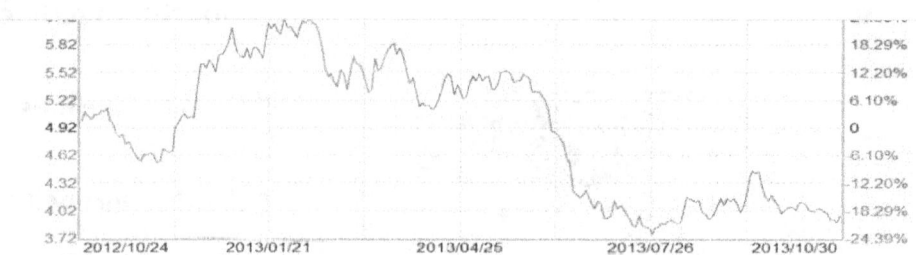

2013

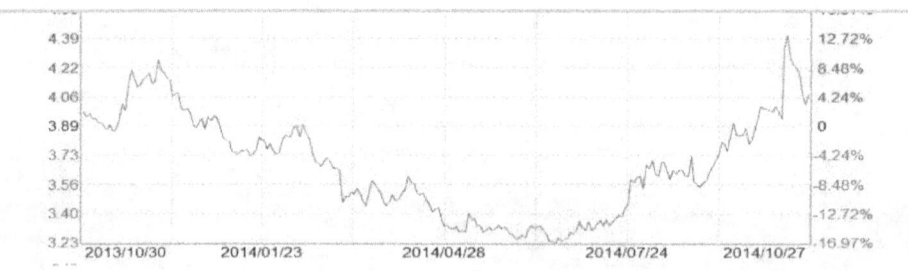

Stock Points = -3 points

Volatility Points = - 1 point

Total Stock Score = -4 points

Total Score All Sections = 8 points = 40%

Recommendation: unacceptable; poor stock performance

Alibaba

Sales

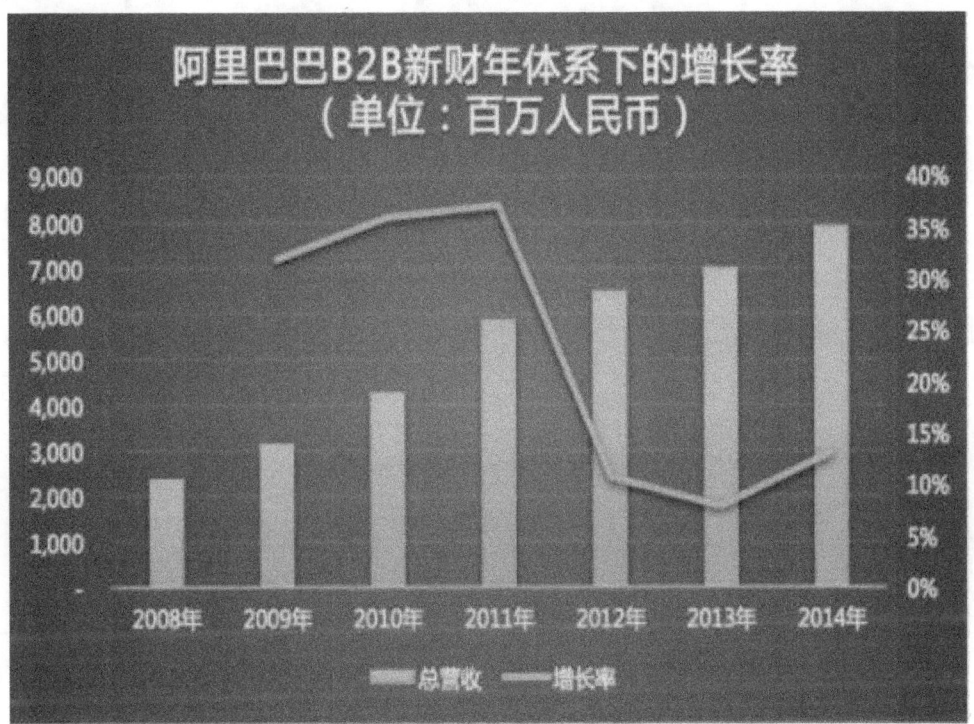

Domestic Sales = 3 points

International = 3 points

Total Score = 6 points

Market Share

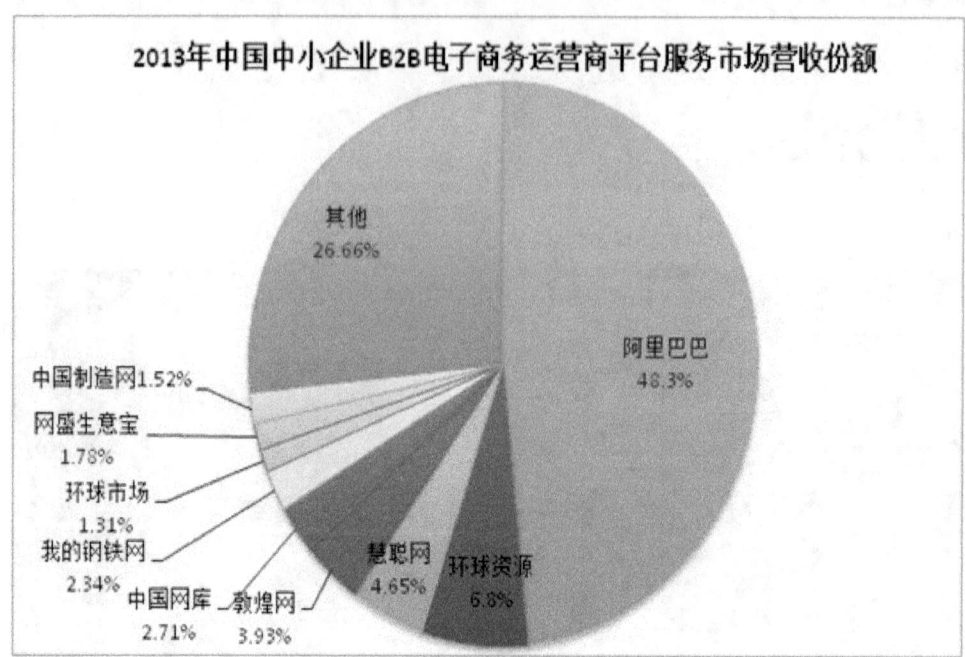

Domestic = 3 points

International = 3 points

Total Score = 6 points

Stock Price

Stock = 0 points

Volatility = -2 points

Total Stock Score = - 2pts

Total Score All Sections = 10 points = 50%

Recommendation: Unacceptable; Stock too volatile (more data required in stock section)

Baidu

Sales

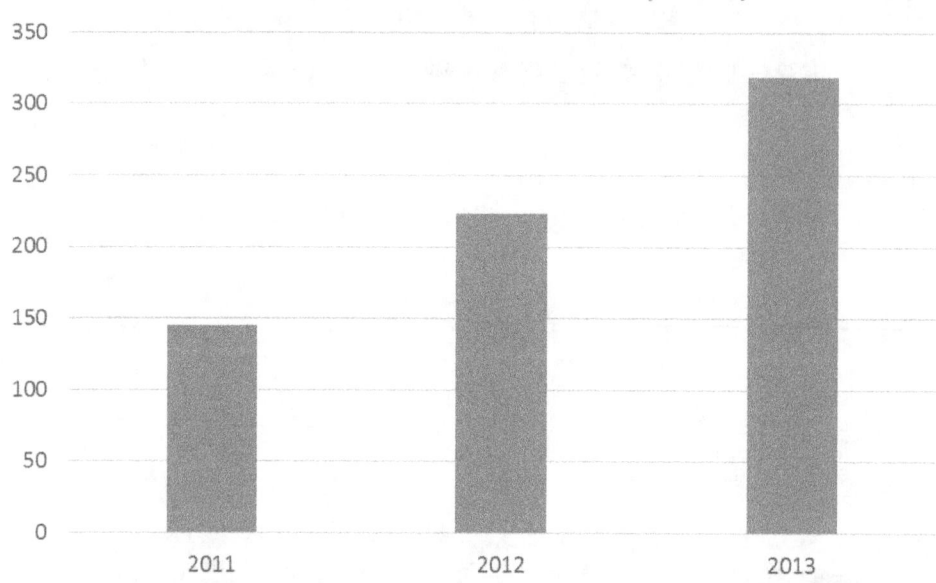

Domestic Sales = 3 points

International Sales = 0 points

Market Share

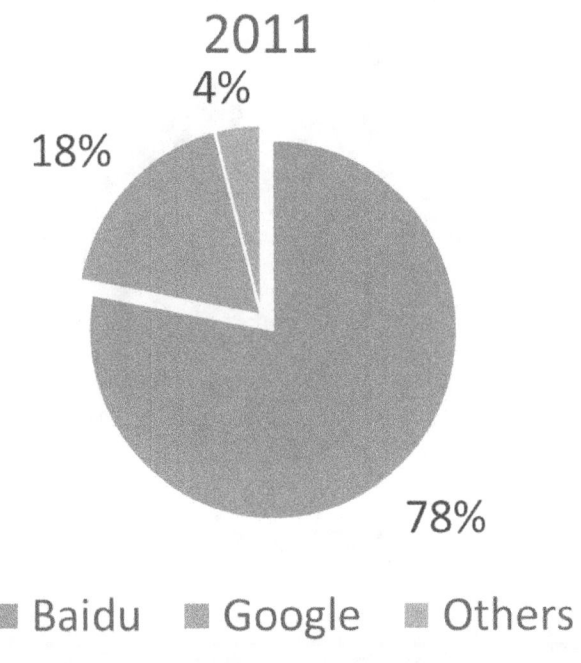

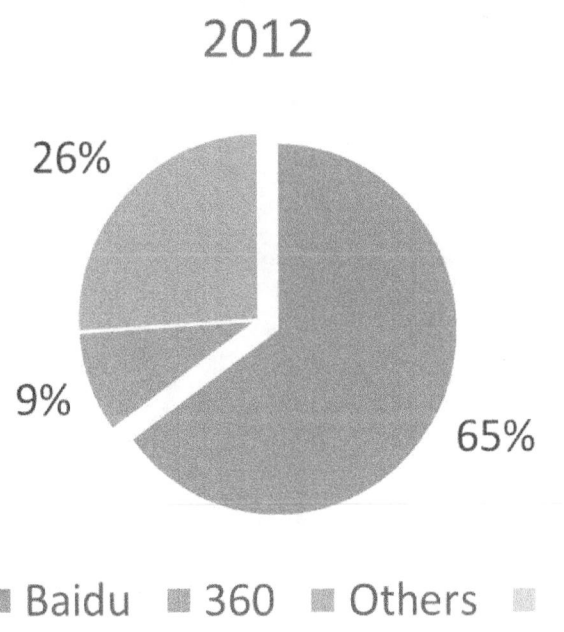

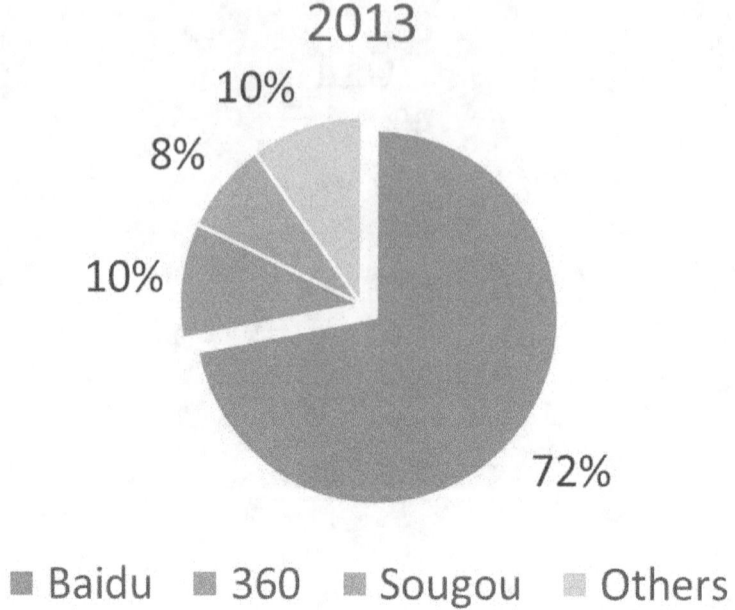

Domestic Market Share Points – 2 pts

International Market Share – 0 pts

Stock Price

Stock Price Points – 3 points

Volatility Points – 3 points

Total Score – All Sections - 11 pts = 55%

Recommendation – Weakness in International Market, but very strong in Chinese Domestic Market; good stock performance in domestic market – Guarded Limited Buy Recommendation

Bank of China

Sales

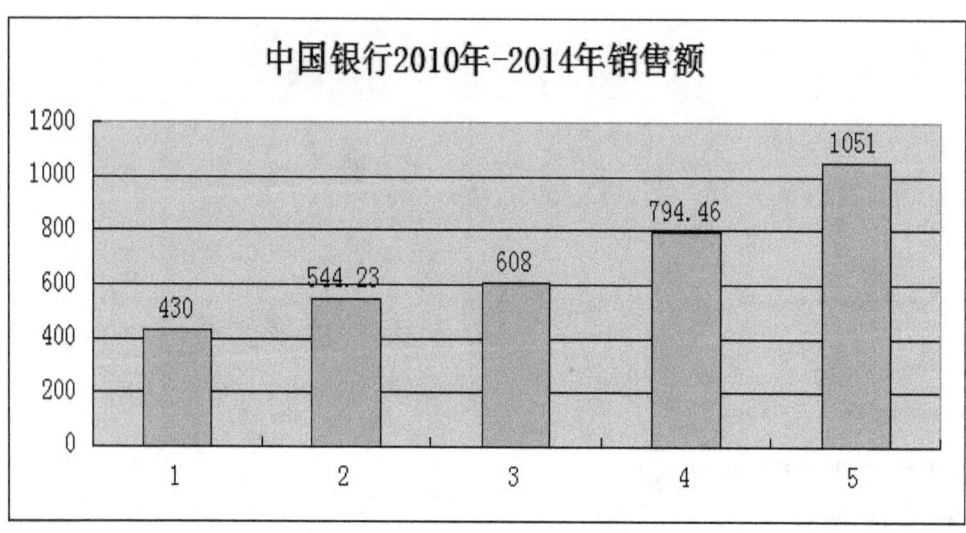

Domestic Sales = 3 points

International Sales = 0 points

Market Share

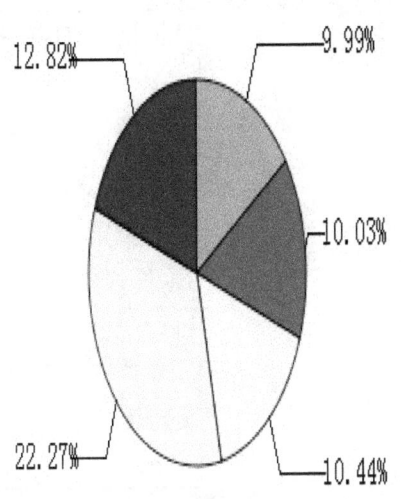

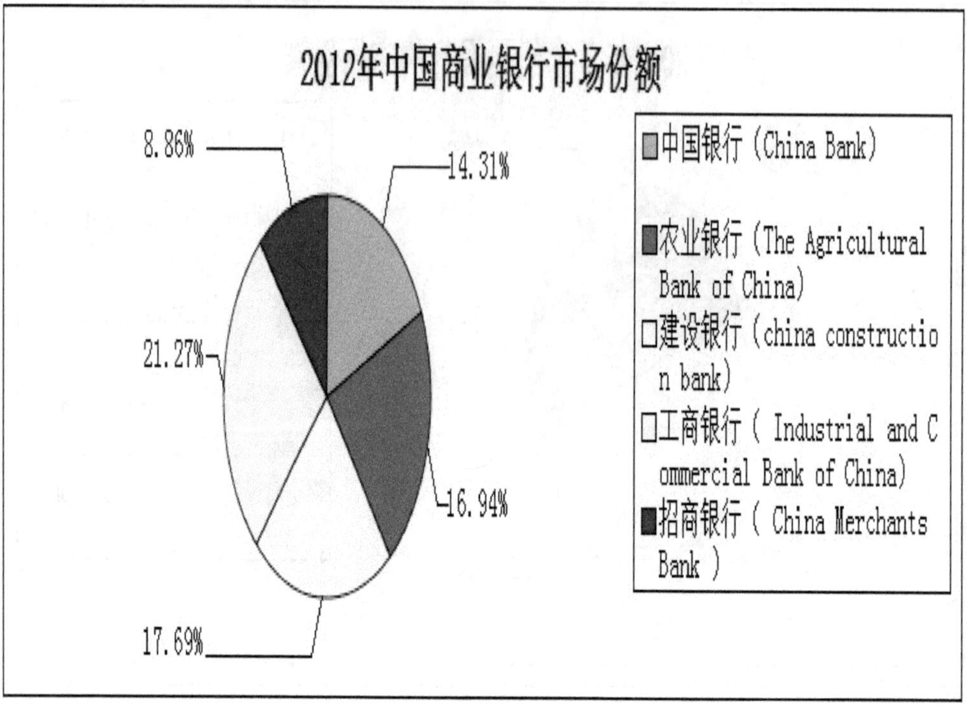

2012年中国商业银行市场份额

- 中国银行(China Bank): 14.31%
- 农业银行(The Agricultural Bank of China): 16.94%
- 建设银行(china construction bank): 17.69%
- 工商银行(Industrial and Commercial Bank of China): 21.27%
- 招商银行(China Merchants Bank): 8.86%

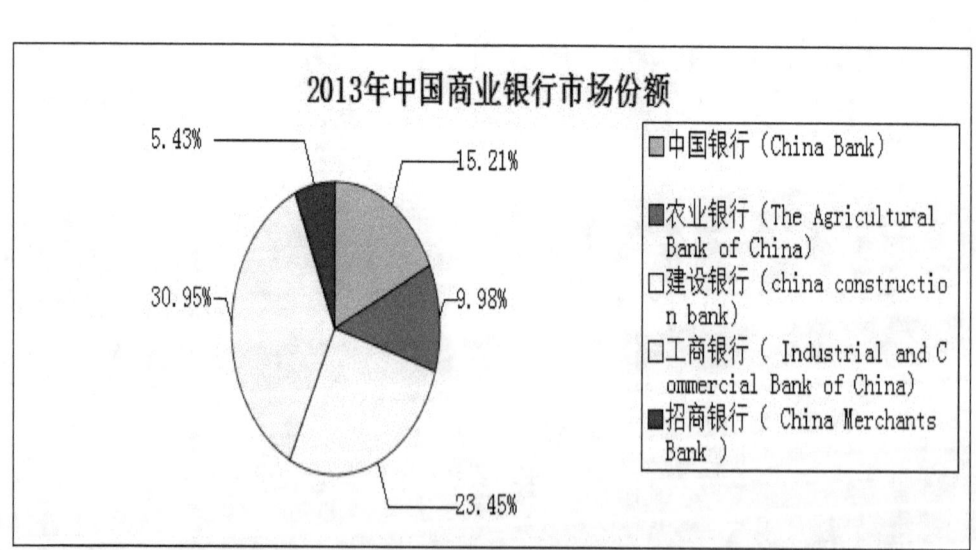

2013年中国商业银行市场份额

- 中国银行(China Bank): 15.21%
- 农业银行(The Agricultural Bank of China): 9.98%
- 建设银行(china construction bank): 23.45%
- 工商银行(Industrial and Commercial Bank of China): 30.95%
- 招商银行(China Merchants Bank): 5.43%

Domestic Market Share – 3 points

International Market Share – 0 points

Stock Price

Stock Price – 0 points

Volatility Rating – 3 points

Total Combined Score – 9 points = 45%

Recommendation – Unacceptable, poor international market sales and market share; poor stock performance

Bank of Communications

Sales

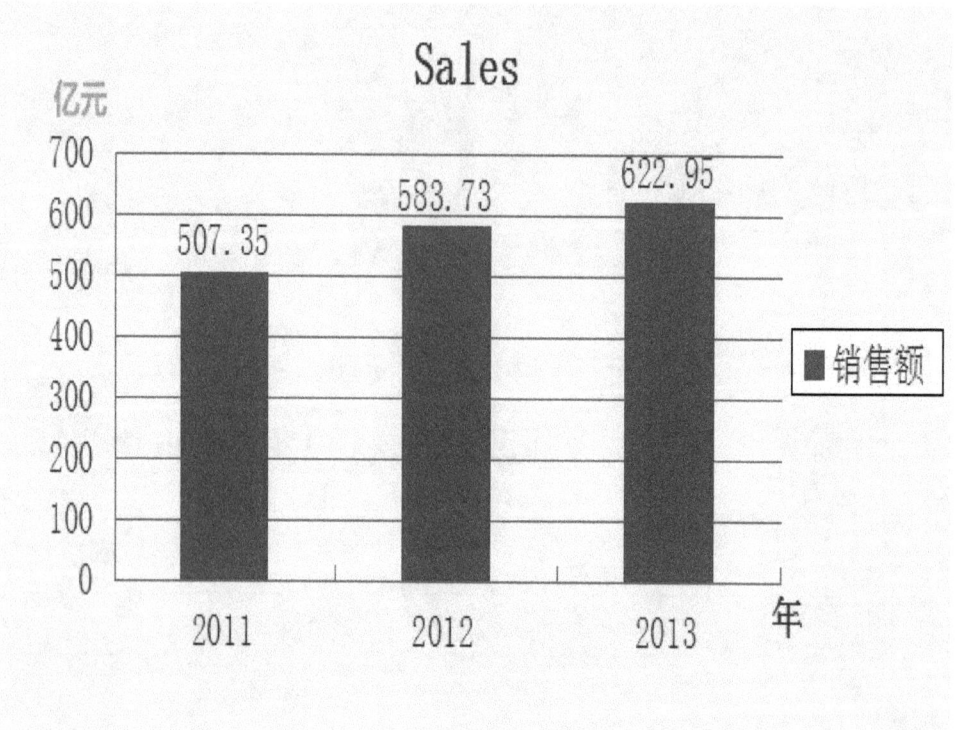

Domestic sales – 3 points

International sales – 0 points

Market Share

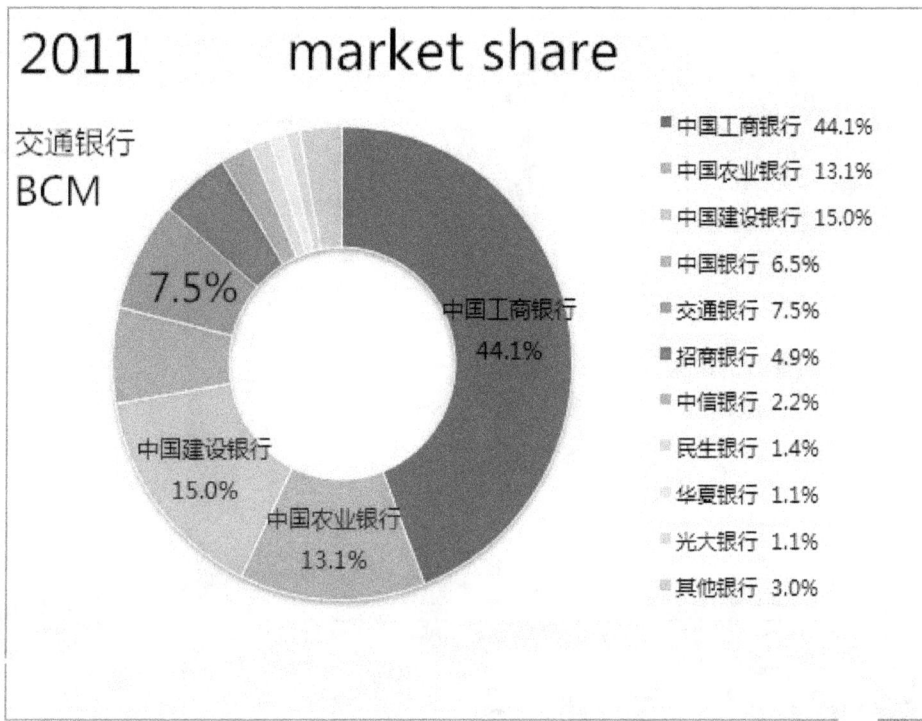

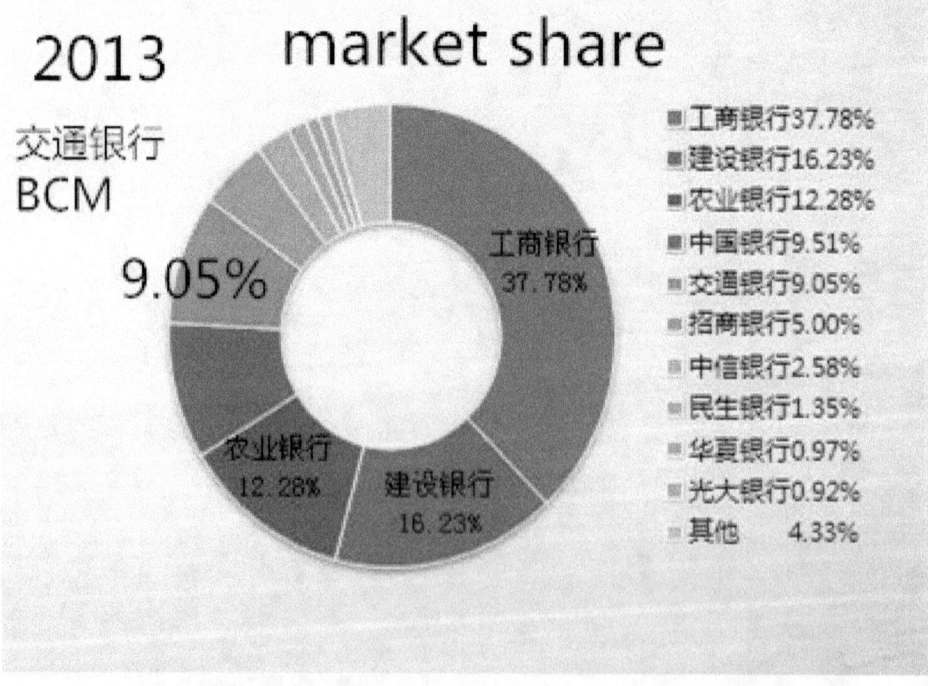

Domestic Market Share – 3 points

International Market Share – 0 points

Stock Price

Stock Price – 0 points

Volatility – 3 points

Total Combined Score - 9 points = 45%

Recommendation: Unacceptable; no international sales, market share, and poor stock performance

China Construction Bank (CCB)

Sales

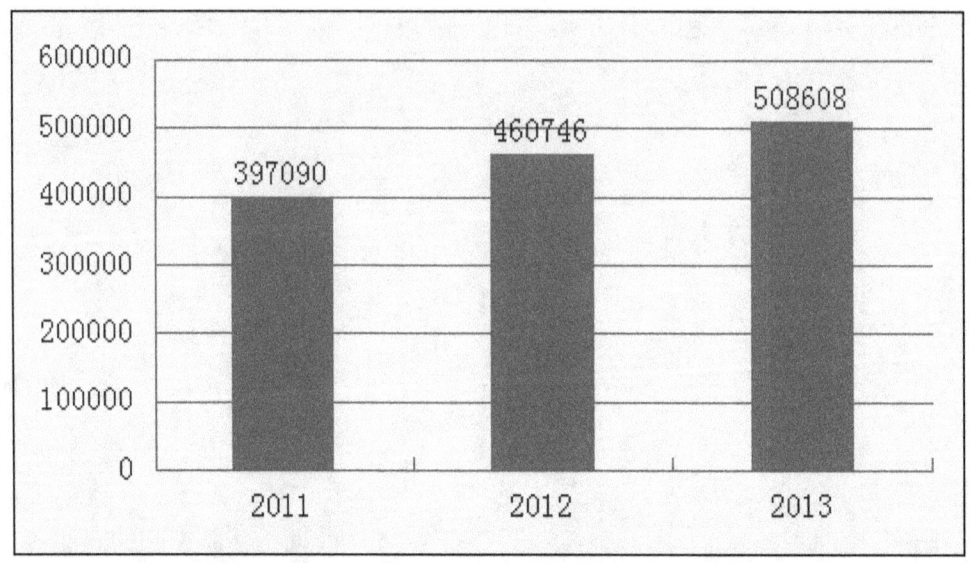

Domestic Sales – 3 points

International Sales – 0 points

Market Share

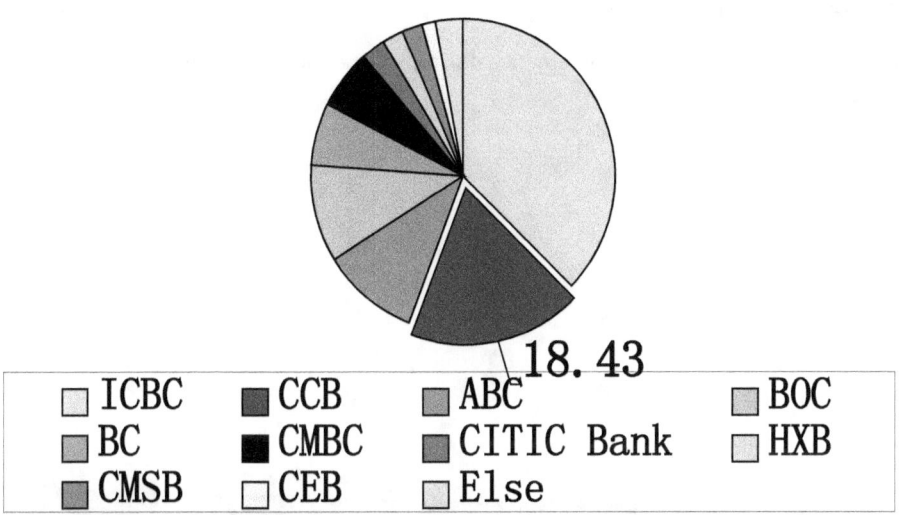

Domestic Market Share – 1 point

International Market Share – 0 points

Stock Price

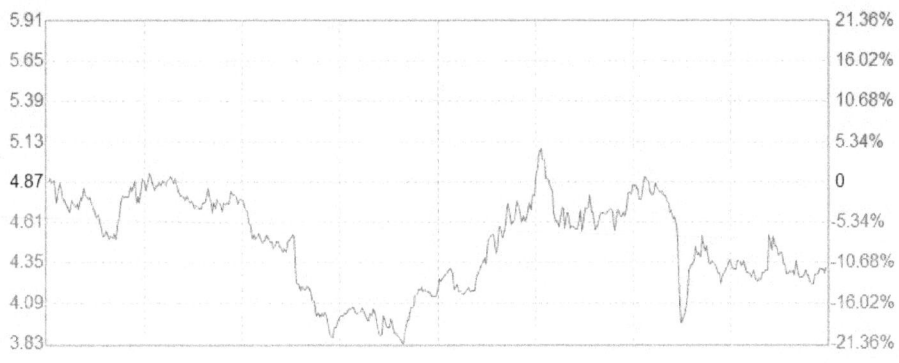

Stock Price – 0 points

Volatility – 3 points

Total Combined Score – 7 points = 35%

Recommendation – Unacceptable – no international sales, no international market share; poor stock performance

CCTV Sales

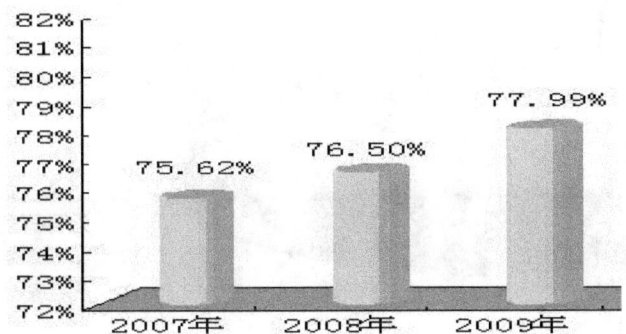

Domestic sales – 3 points

International Sales – 1 point

Market Share

2011

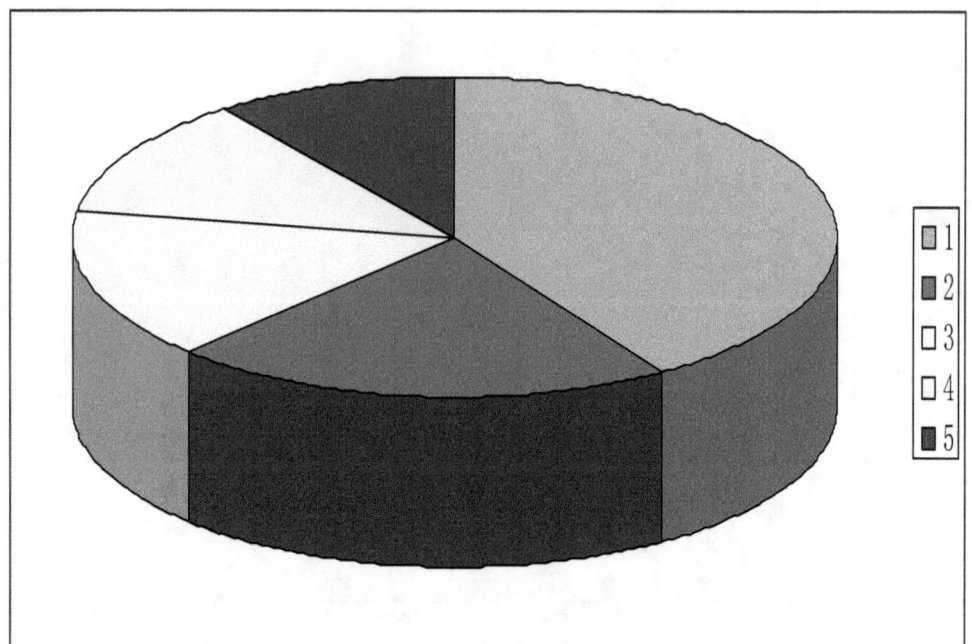

1- CCTV 40%
2- Hunan TV 21%
3- Zhejiang TV 15%
4- Shenzhen TV 12%
5- Beijing TV 12%

2012

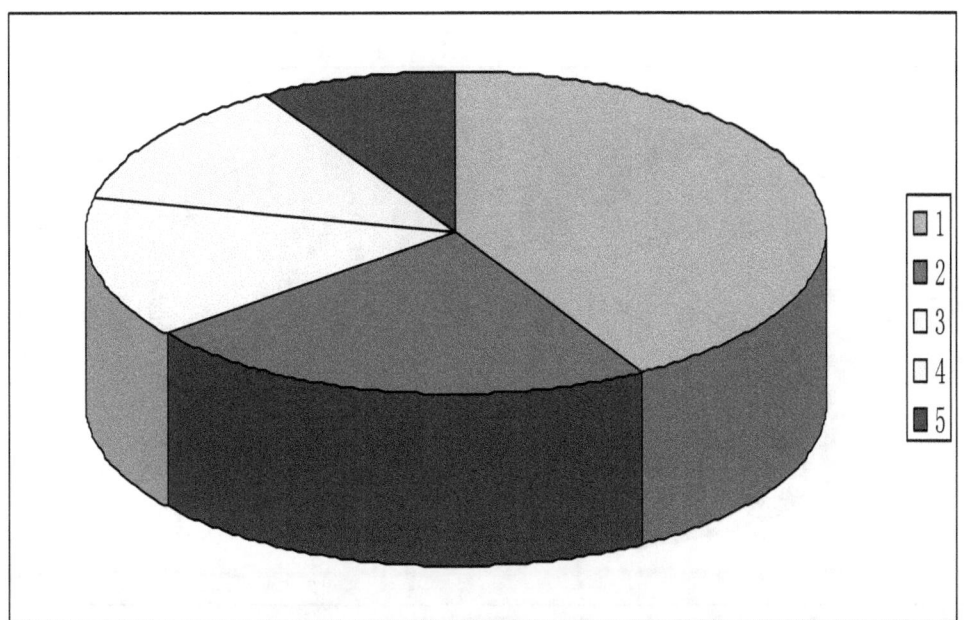

CCTV – 45%

2013

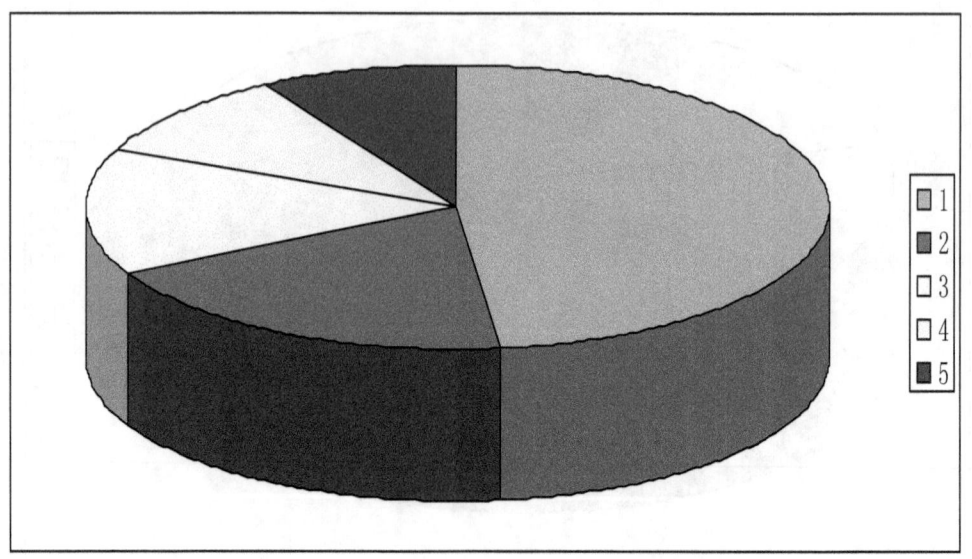

CCTV 49%

Domestic Market Share – 3 points

International Market Share – 1 point

Stock Price

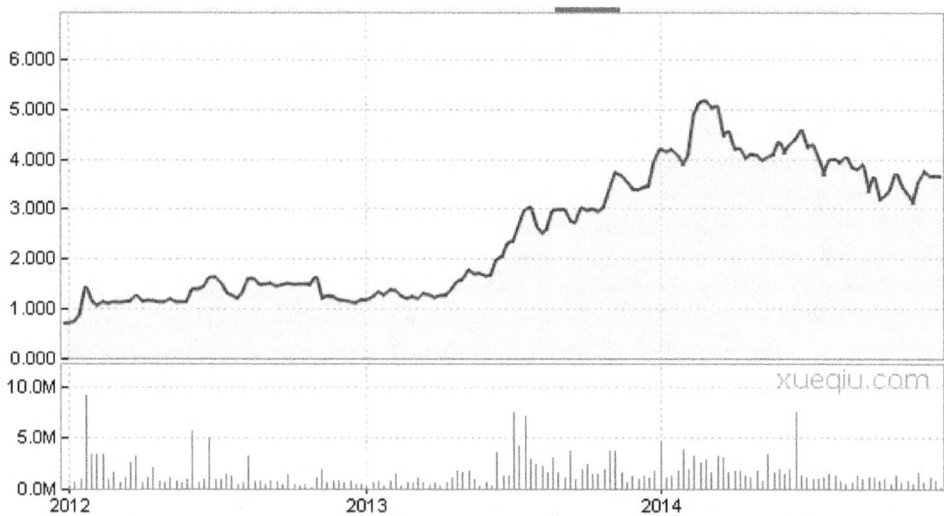

Stock Price – 2 points

Volatility – 3 points

Total Combined Score – 13 points = 65%

Recommendation: Guarded Buy: Weak International Market, but good domestic

performance in sales, market share and stock price.

China Industrial Bank
Sales

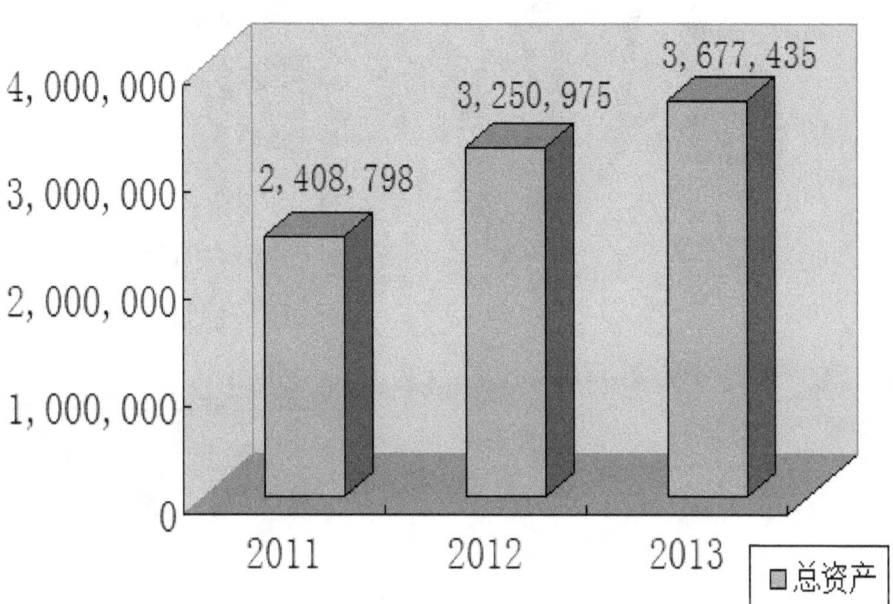

Domestic Sales – 3 points

International Sales – 0 points

Market Share

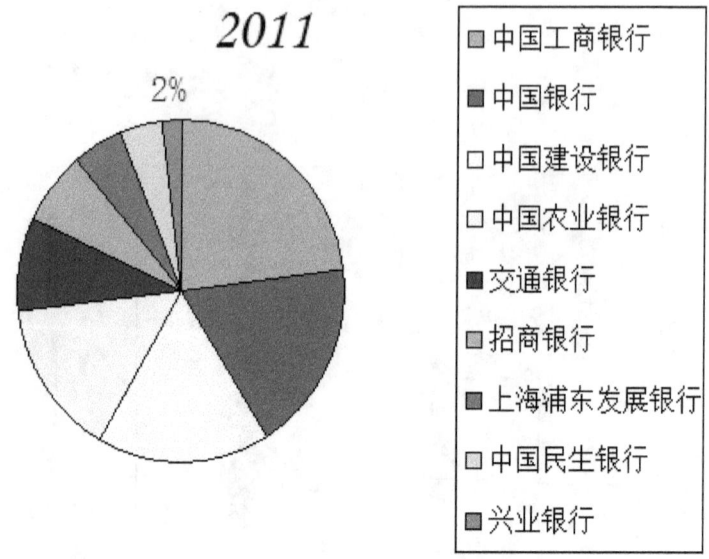

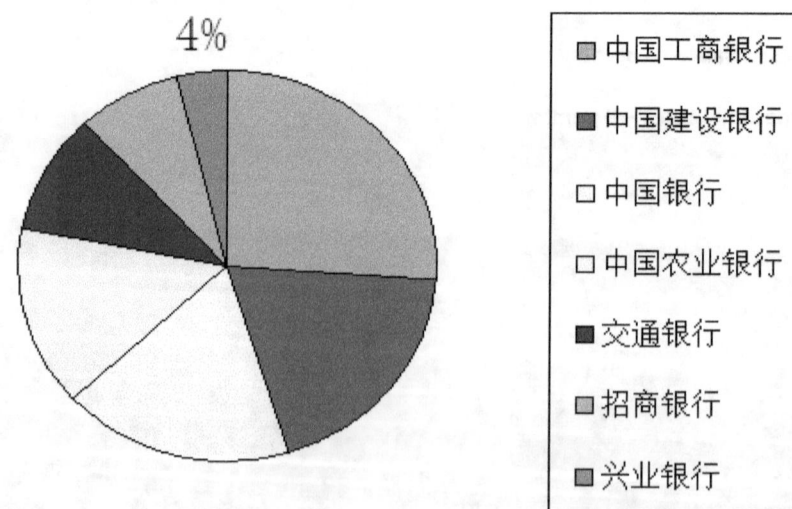

Chinese Commercial Bank 2013

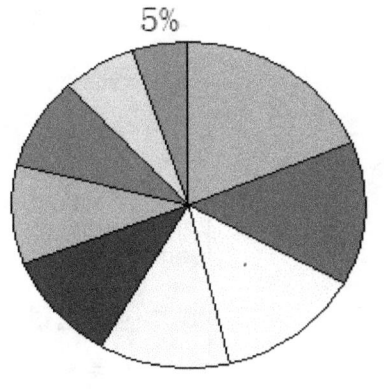

- 中国工商银行
- 中国建设银行
- 中国银行
- 中国农业银行
- 交通银行
- 招商银行
- 中国中信银行
- 上海浦东发展银行
- 兴业银行

Domestic Market Share – 3 points

International Market Share – 0 points

Stock Price

Chinese Commercial Bank 2013

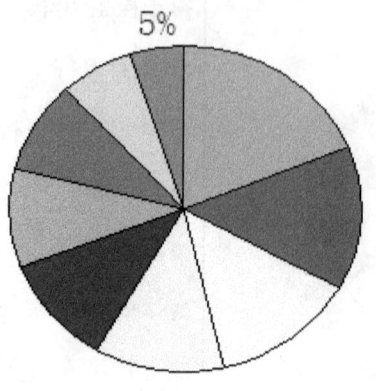

- 中国工商银行
- 中国建设银行
- 中国银行
- 中国农业银行
- 交通银行
- 招商银行
- 中国中信银行
- 上海浦东发展银行
- 兴业银行

Stock Price

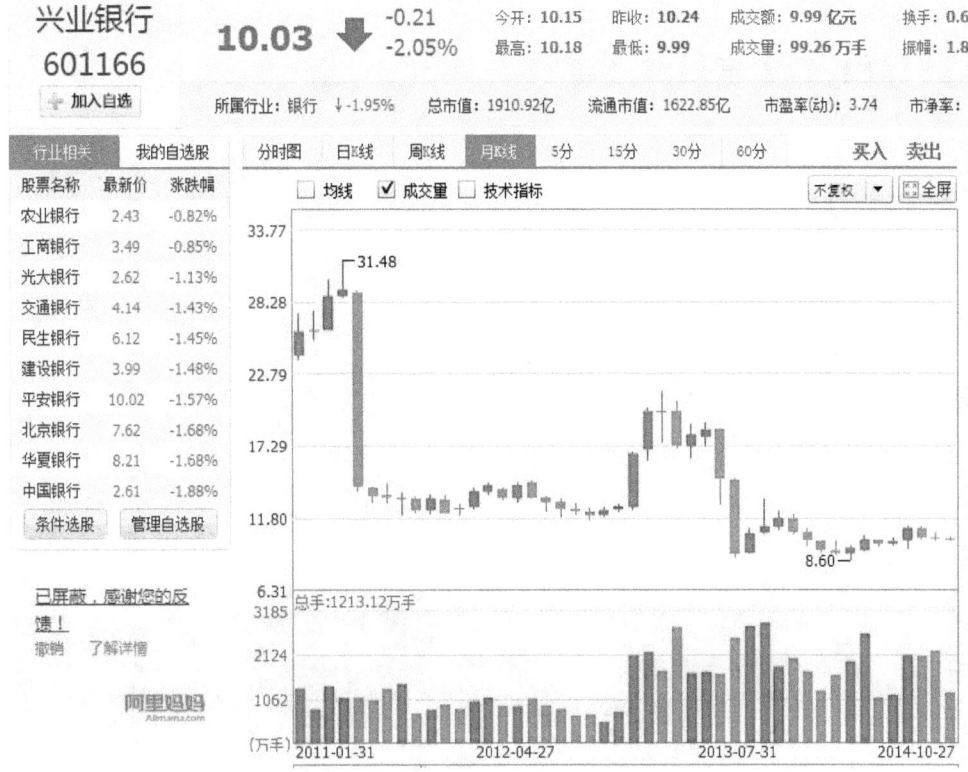

Stock Price – 0 points

Volatility – 0 points

Total Combined Score – 6 points = 30%

Recommendation – Unacceptable – no international sales, market share; poor stock performance, volatile

China Telecom Sales

Domestic Sales – 3 points

International Sales – 0 points

Market Share

Domestic Market Share – 3 points

International Market Share – 0 points

Stock Price – 0 points

Volatility – 3 points

Total Combined Score -   9 points – 45%

Recommendation – Unacceptable – No international sales or market share; poor stock performance

China Mobile Sales

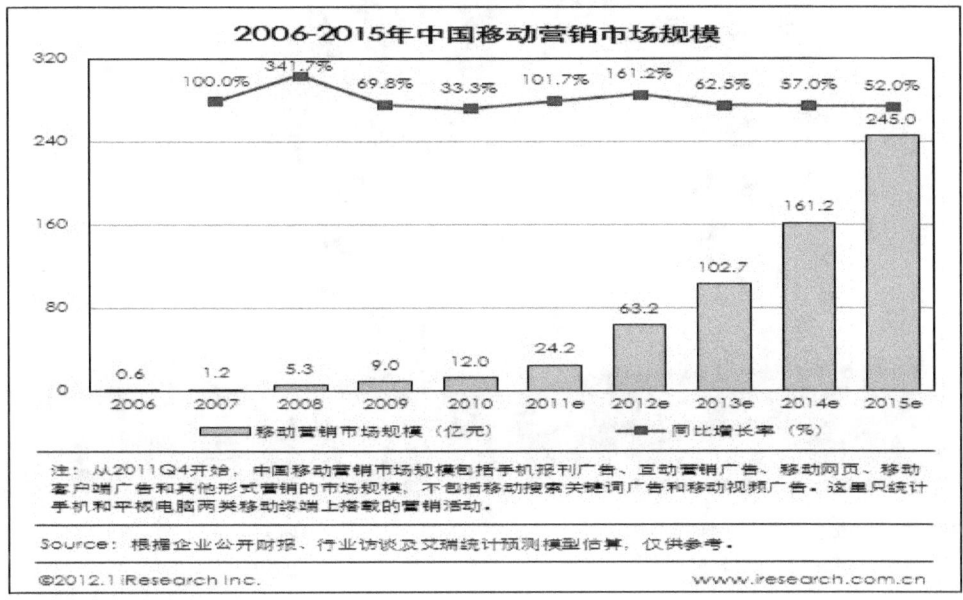

Domestic sales – 3 points

International sales – 1 point

Market Share

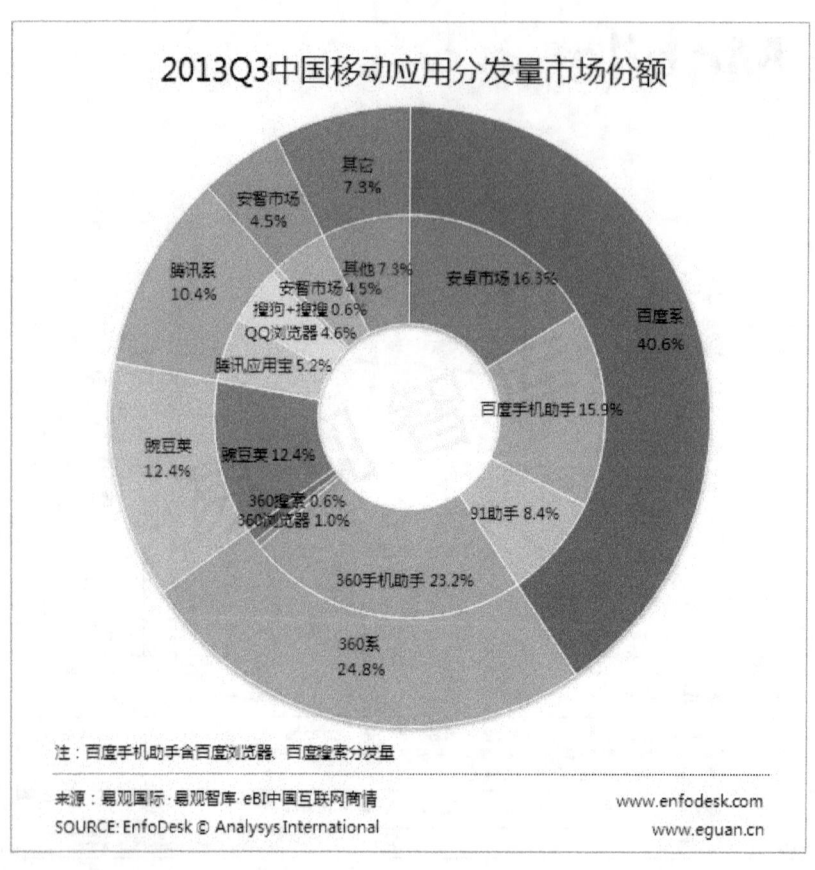

Domestic Market Share – 3 points

International Market Share – 1 point

Stock Price

中国移动通信集团公司[CHL] 美股实时行情 新浪财经

58.36 ↑ +1.37 (+2.40%)

2014-10-24 16:00:00 (美东时间)

今开：57.73　最高：58.69　成交量：76.63万　道琼斯：16805.41 (+0.76%)
昨收：56.99　最低：57.38　市盈率：12.52　纳斯达克：4483.71 (+0.69%)

Stock price – 1 point

Volatility - 3 points

Total Combined Score - 12 points – 60%

Recommendation: guarded buy, but soft in international sales and market share

China Petro

Sales

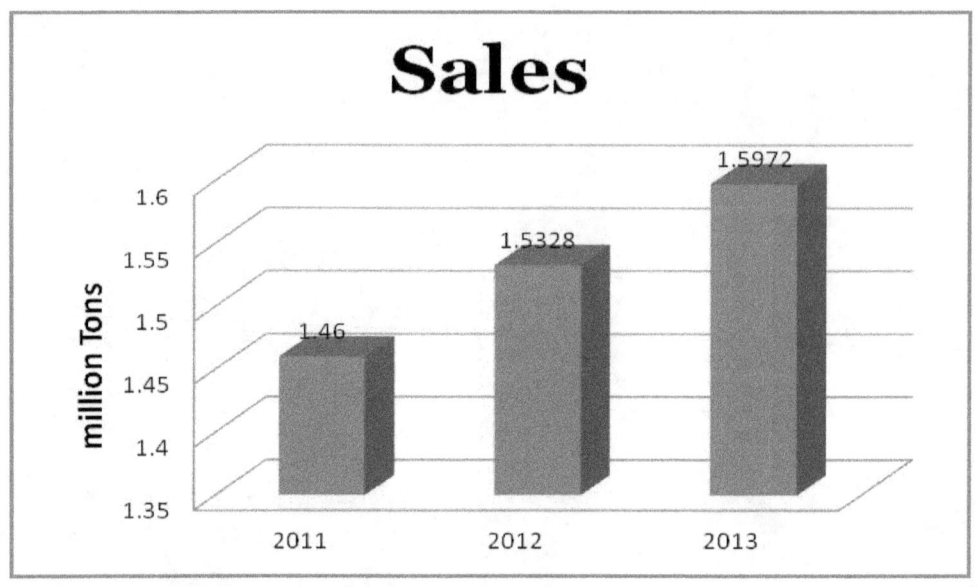

Domestic sales – 3 points

International sales – 1 point

Market Share

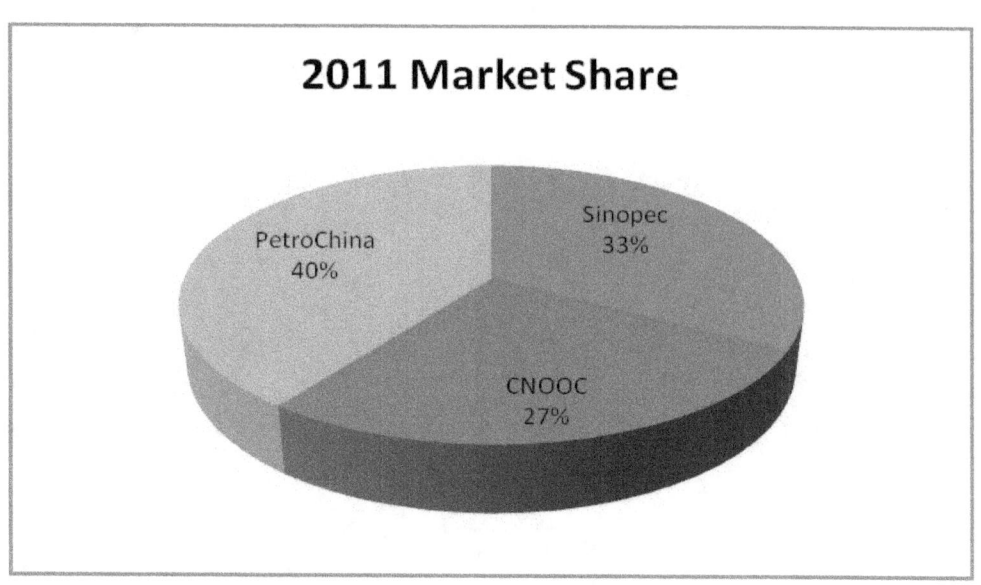
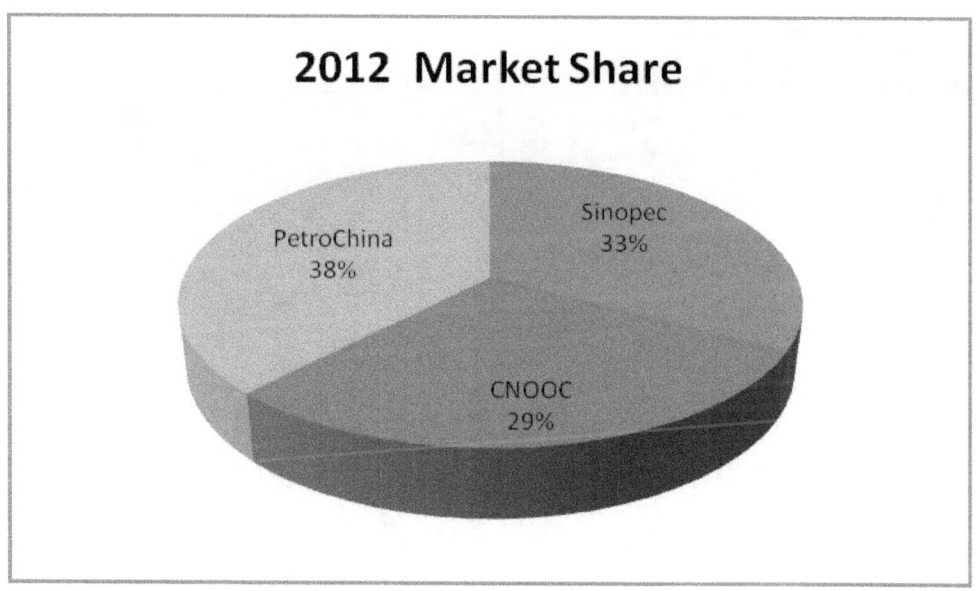

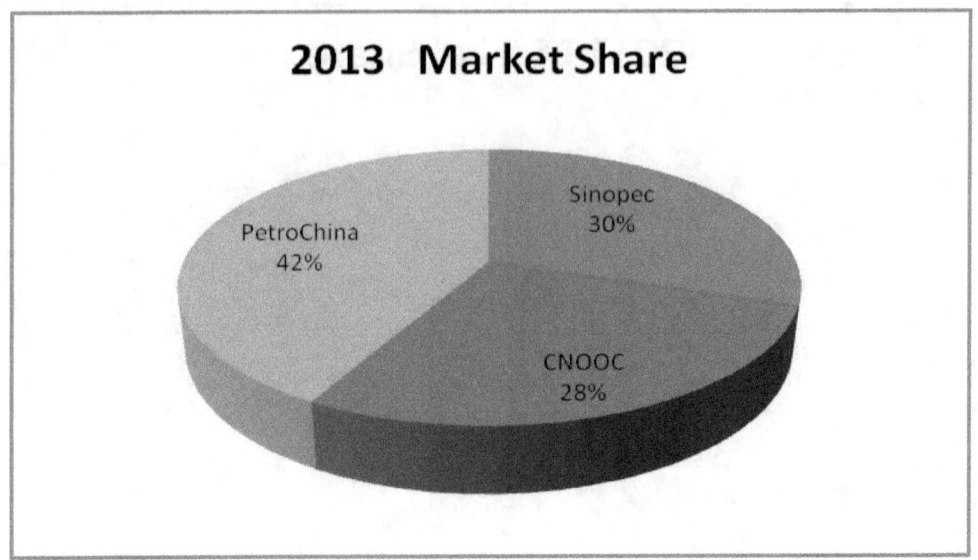

Domestic market share – 1 point

International Market share – 1 point

Stock Price

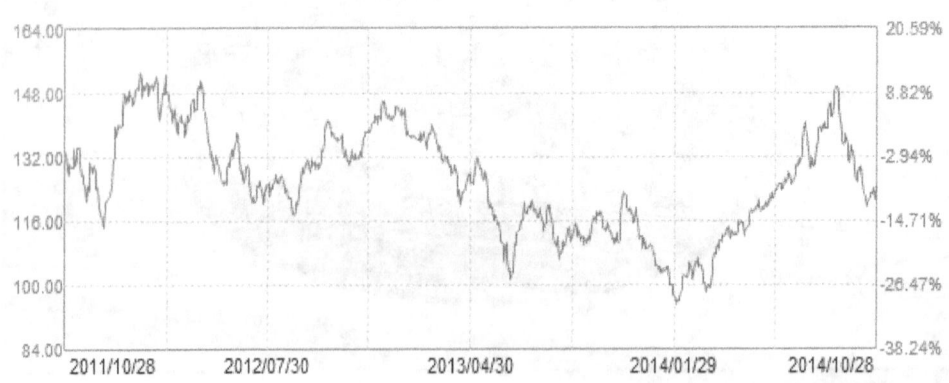

Stock price – 0 points

Volatility – 2 points

Total Combined Score – 8 points – 40%

Recommendation – Unacceptable – low international sales and market share; poor stock performance

China Post

Sales

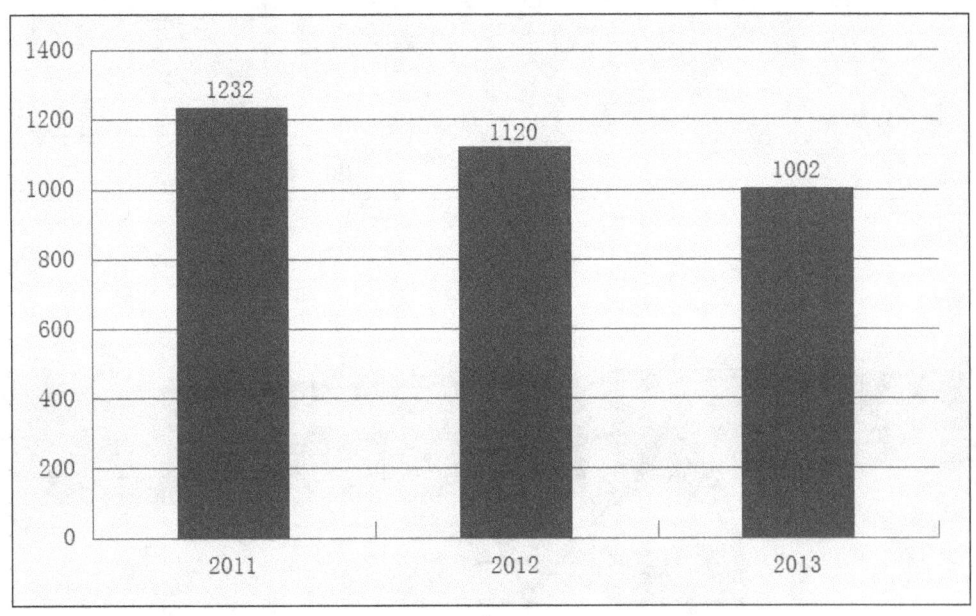

Domestic sales – 0 points

International sales – 0 points

Market Share

2011

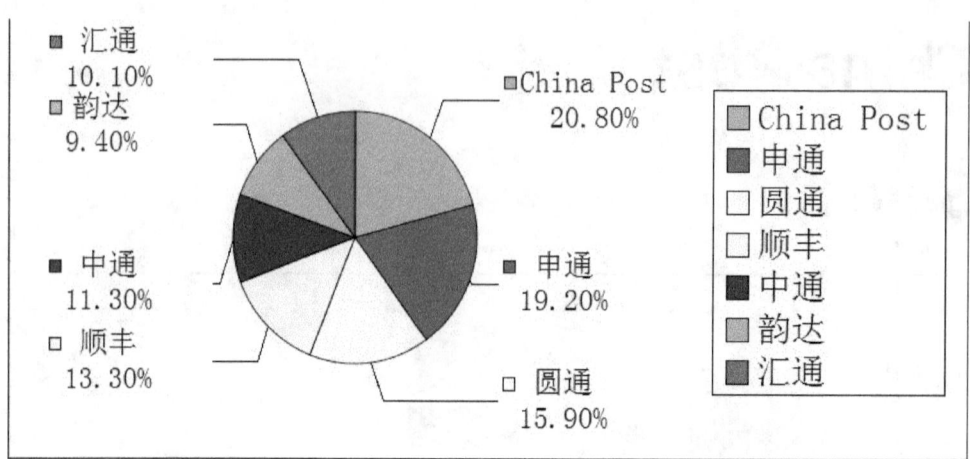

2012

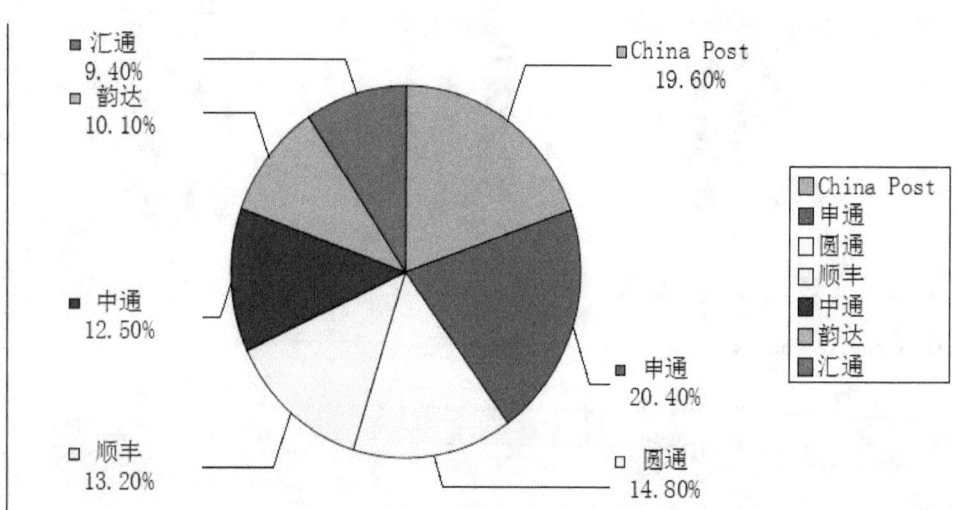

2013

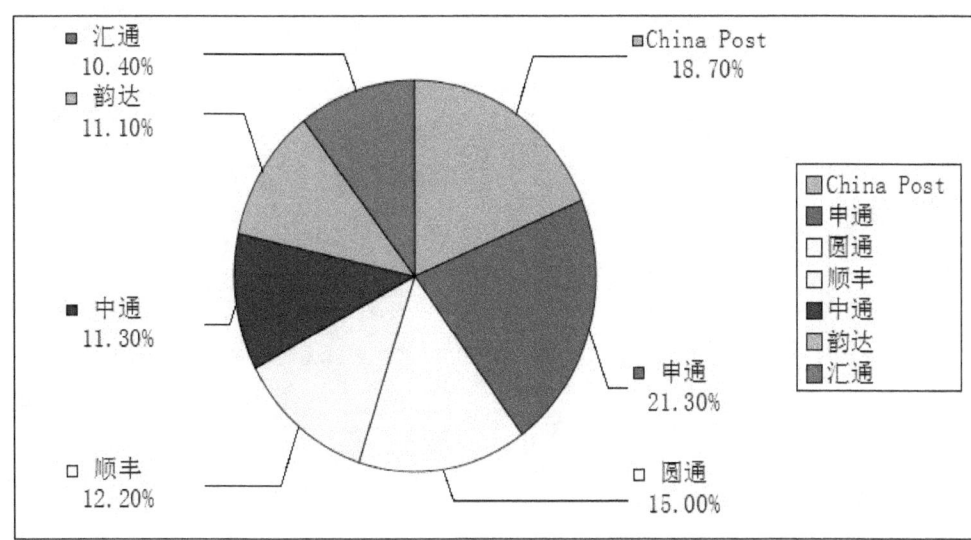

Domestic Market Share – 0 points

International Market Share – 0 points

Stock Price

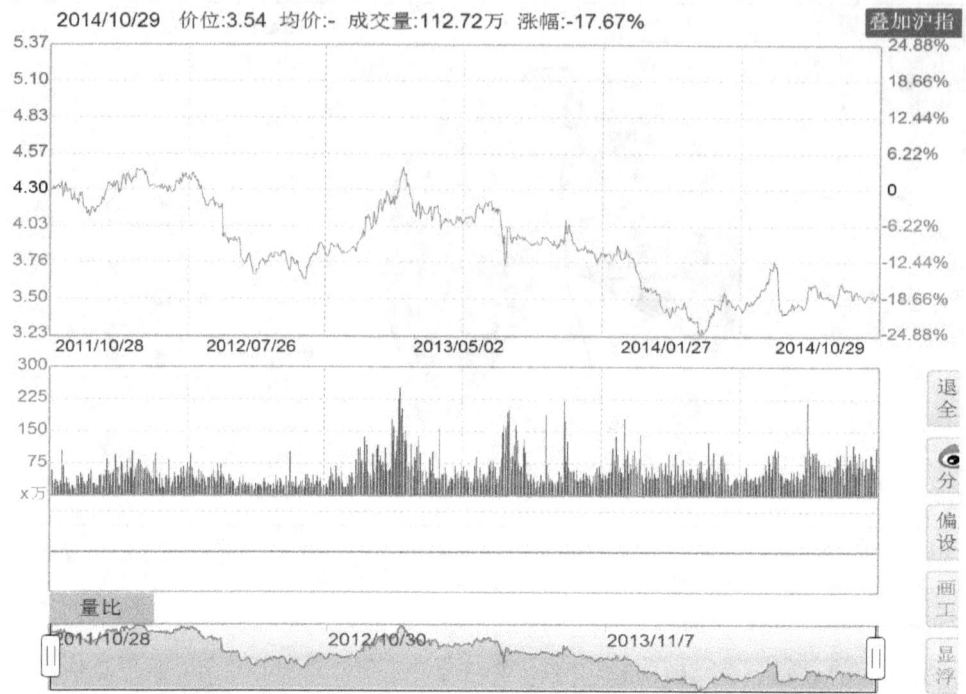

Stock price – 0 points

Volatility – 3 points

Total Combined Score – 3 points – 15%

Recommendation – Unacceptable – Losing Domestic Sales and Market Share; poor stock performance

China Merchants Bank Sales

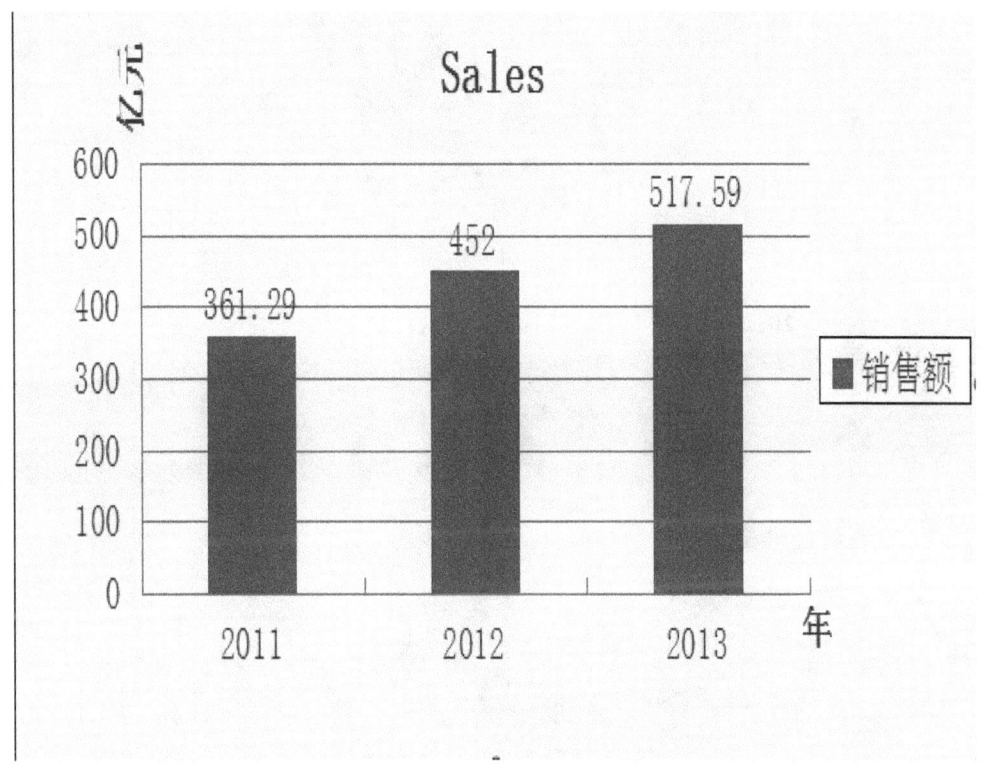

Domestic Sales – 3 points

International Sales – 0 points

Market Share 2011 – 4.9

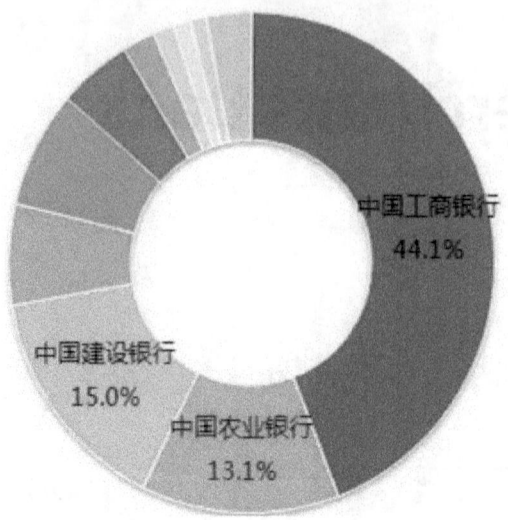

2012 – 4.3

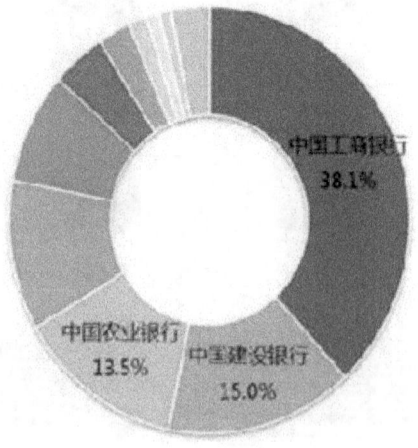

2013 – 5.2

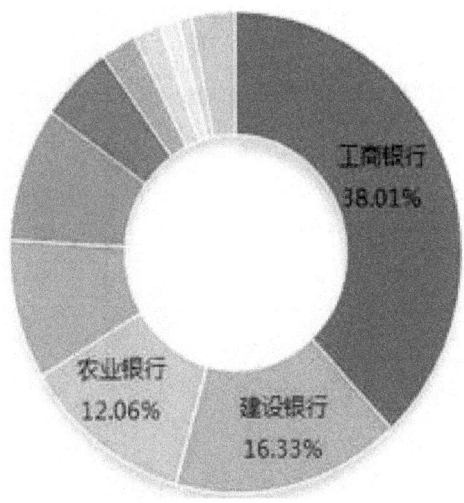

Domestic Market Share – 1 point

International Market Share – 0 points

Stock Price

Stock Price – 0 points

Volatility – 3 points

Total Combined Score – 7 points = 35%

Recommendation: Unacceptable; no international sales or market share; poor stock performance

China Minsheng Banking Sales

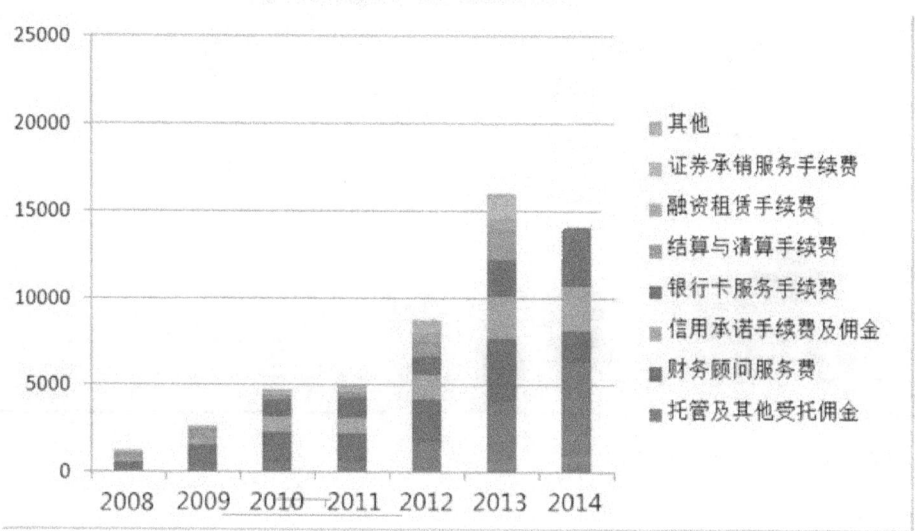

domestic sales – 2 points

International sales – 0 points

Market Share

Domestic market share – 1 point

International market share – 0 points

Stock price

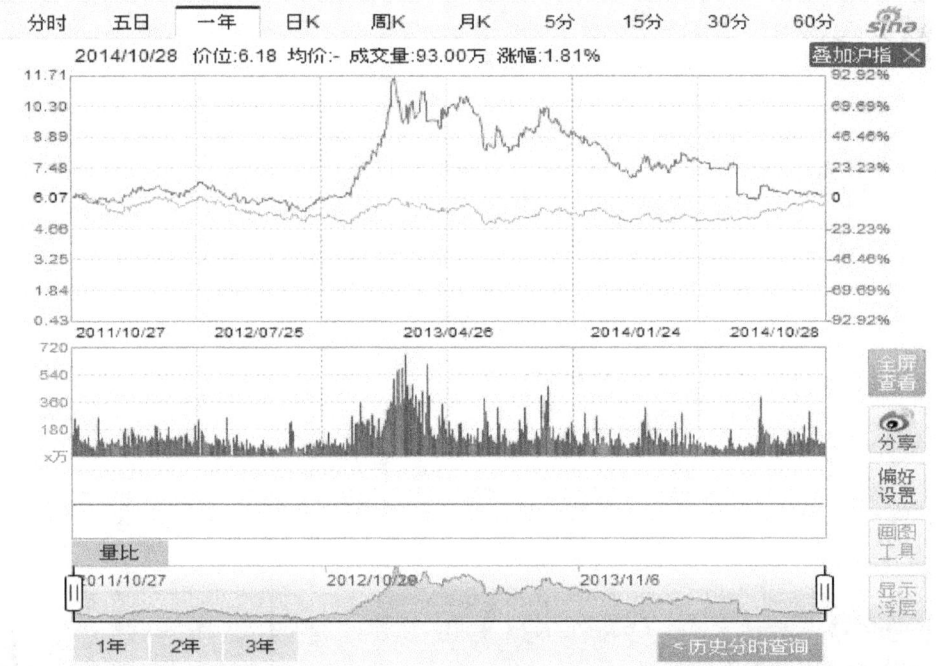

Stock price- 1 point

Volatility – 3 points

Total Combined Score – 7 points – 35%

Recommendation – Unacceptable – no international sales or market share

Dicos
Sales

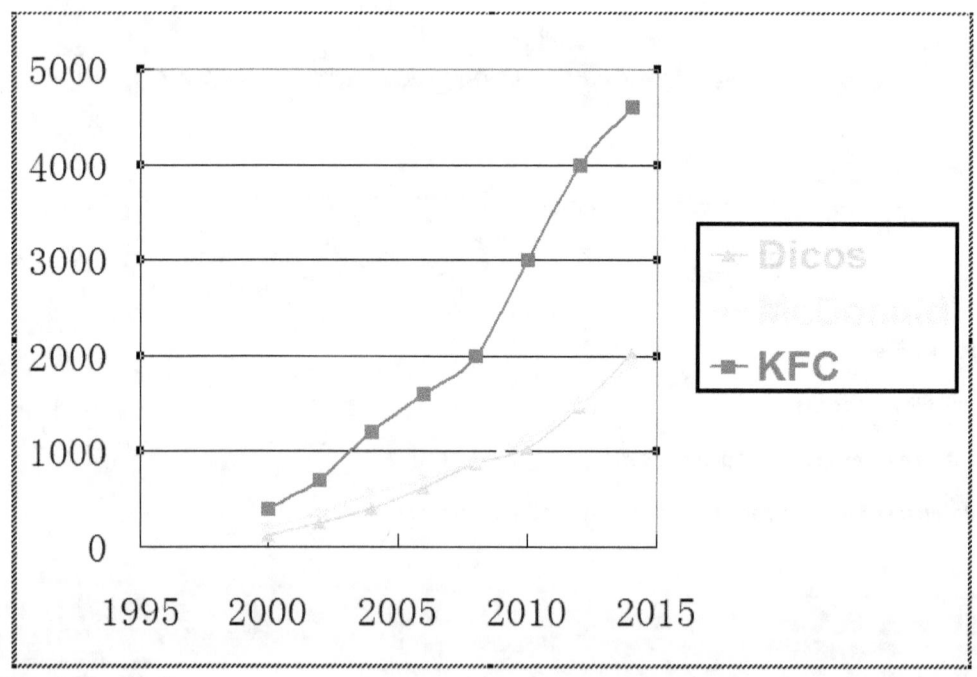

Domestic sales – 3 points

International sales – 1 point

Market Share

Domestic Market Share – 3 points

International Market Share – 0 points

Stock Price - 0 points

Volatility – 3 points

Total Combined Score – 10 points = 50%

Recommendation: Unacceptable; no international market share; poor stock performance

Geely

Sales

	2011/12/1	2012/12/1	2013/12/1		
	430000	480000	560000		
				600000	

Domestic sales – 3 points

International sales – 1 point

Domestic Market Share - 3 points

International Market Share – 1 point

Stock price

Stock price – 1 point

Volatility – 3 points

Total Combined Score – 12 pts – 60%

Recommendation – guarded buy, weak in international market share, but domestic sales good and stock performance ok

Gome Sales

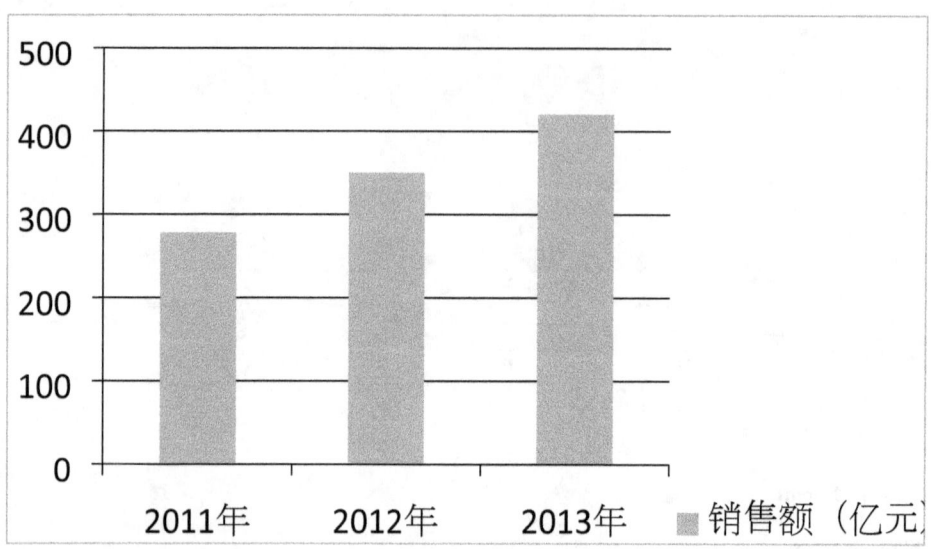

Domestic sales – 3 points

International sales – 0 points

Market Share

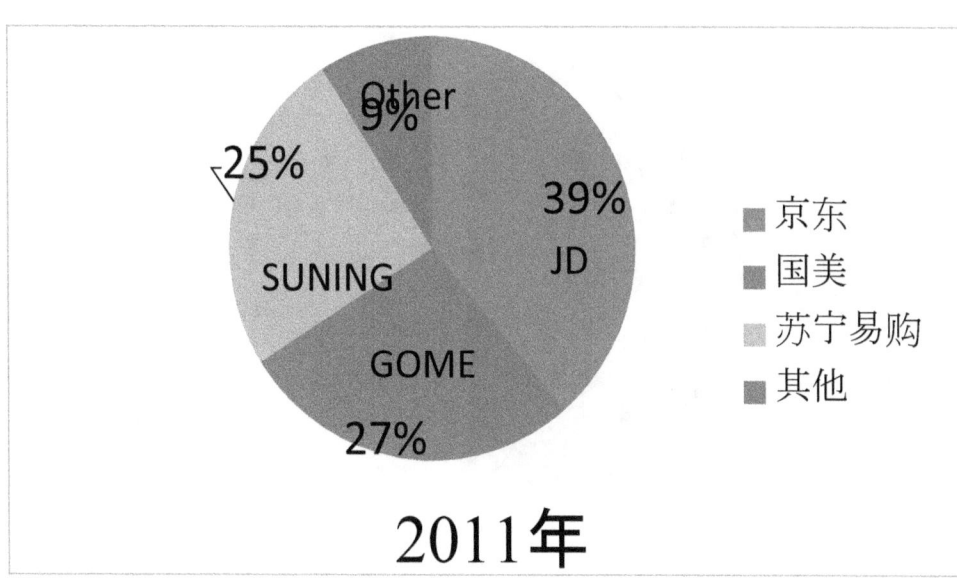

2011年

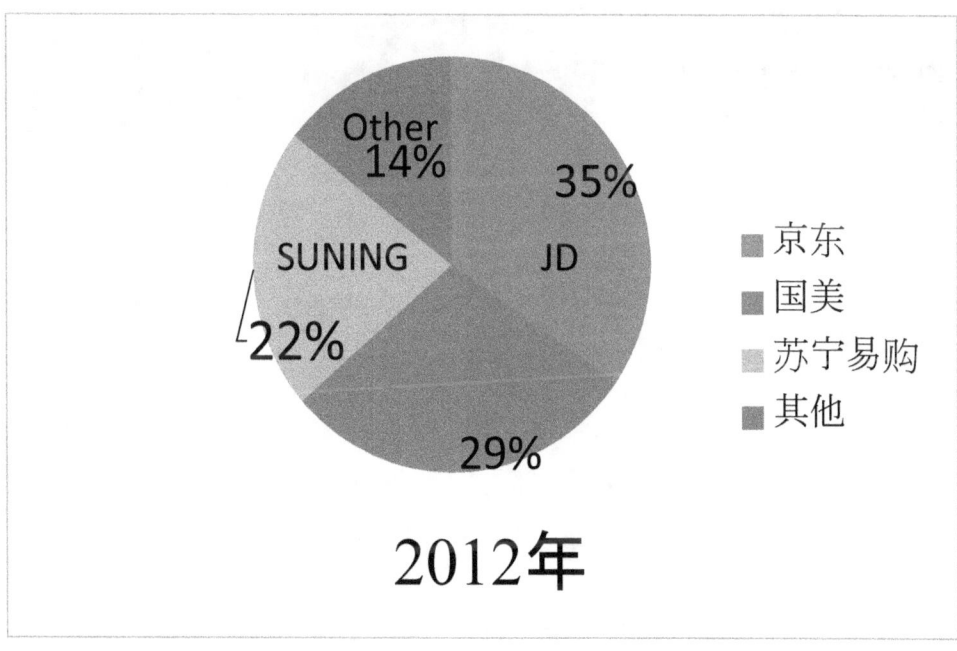

2012年

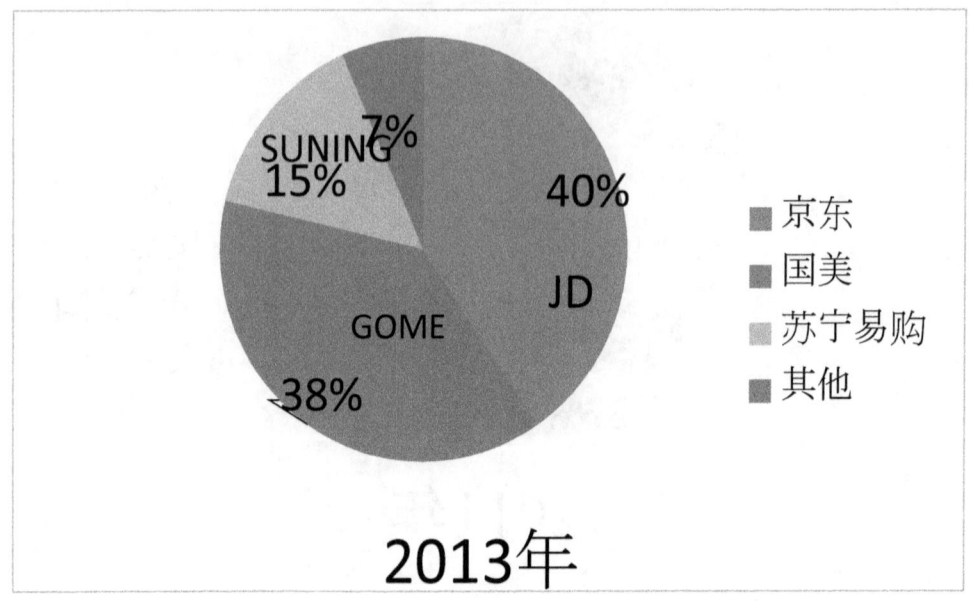

Domestic market share – 3 points

International sales – 0 points

Stock Price

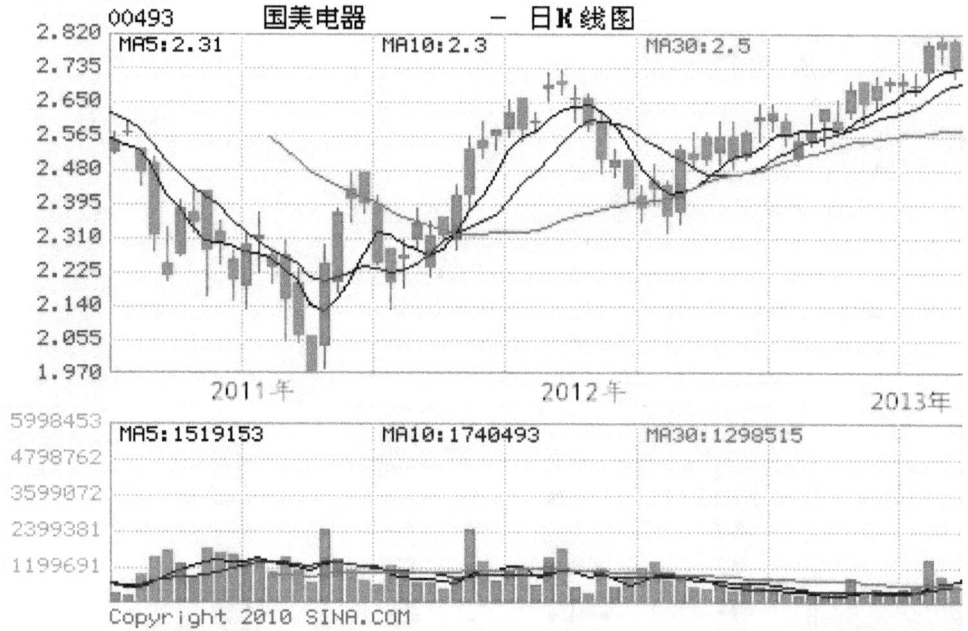

Stock price – 2 points

Volatility – 2 points

Total Combined Score 10 points – 50%

Recommendation: Unacceptable; poor international market share and shaky stock

Great Wall Sales

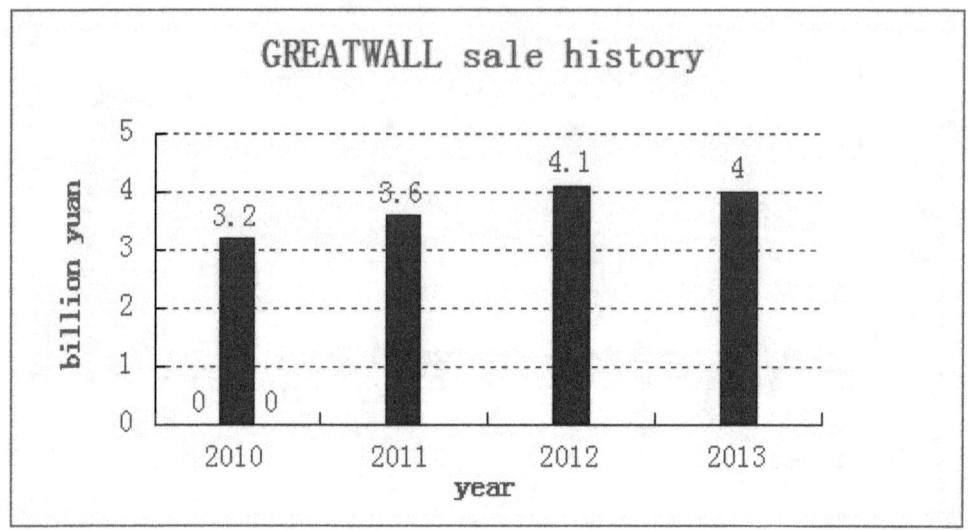

Domestic sales – 3 points

International sales – 1 point

Market Share

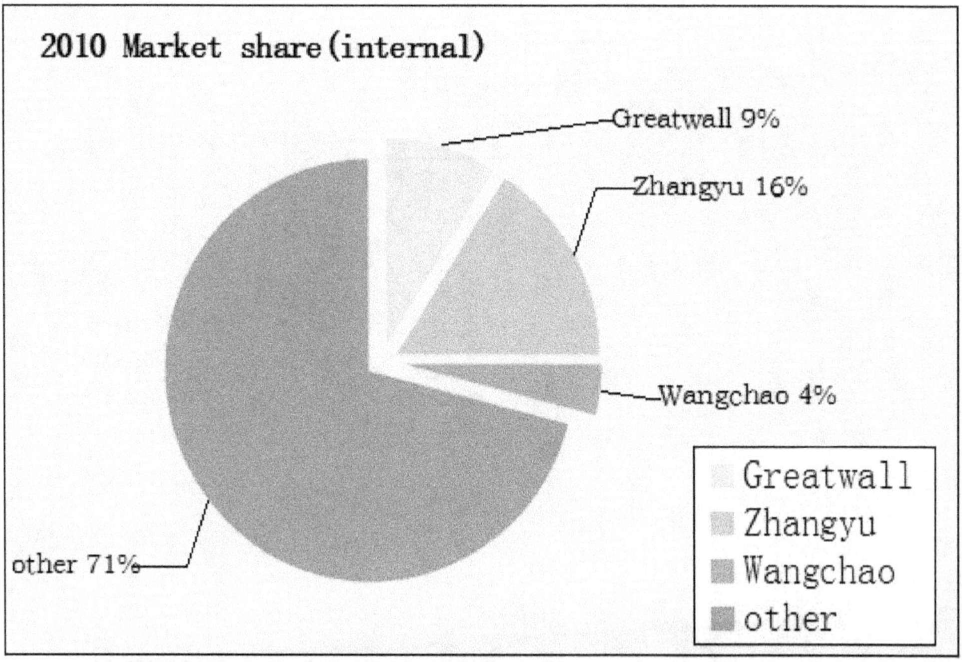
2010 Market share(internal)
Greatwall 9%
Zhangyu 16%
Wangchao 4%
other 71%
Greatwall
Zhangyu
Wangchao
other

2011 Market share(internal)
Greatwall 10%
Zhangyu 17%
Wangchao 5%
other 68%
Greatwall
Zhangyu
Wangchao
other

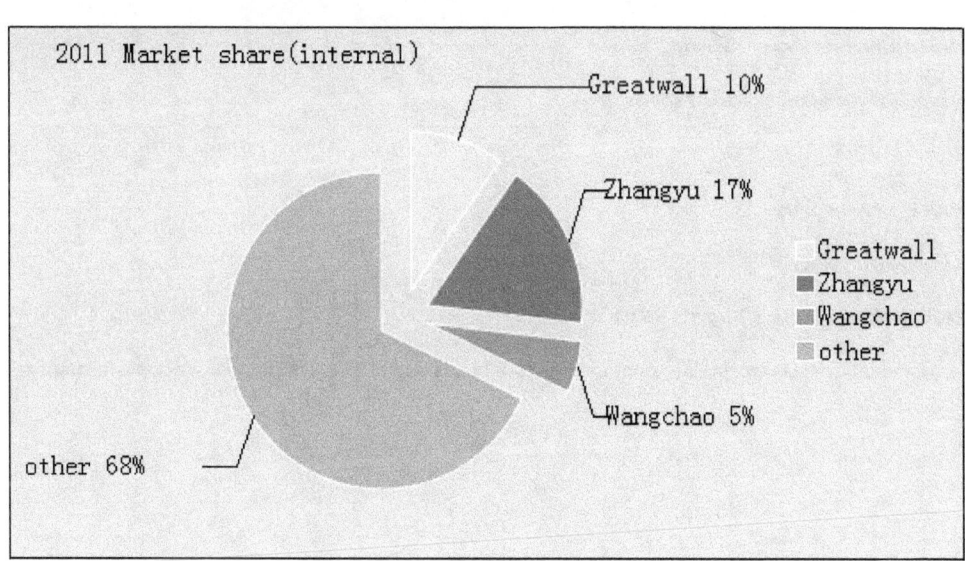

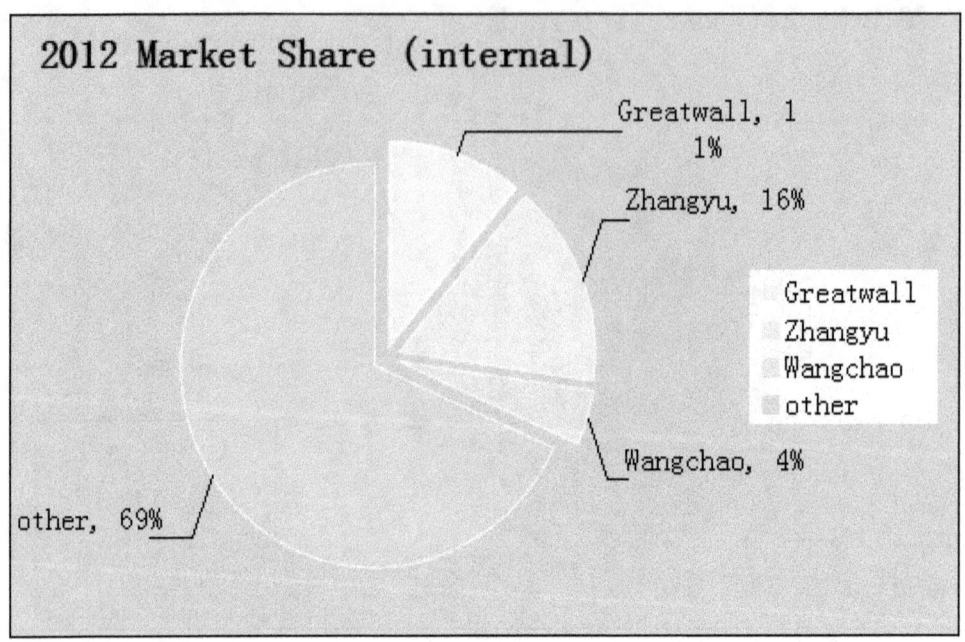

Domestic market share – 3 points

International market share – 0 points

Stock Price – 0 points

Volatility – 0 points

Total Combined Score - 7 points – 35%

Recommendation: Unacceptable; poor international sales and market share; poor stock performance

Home Inn Sales

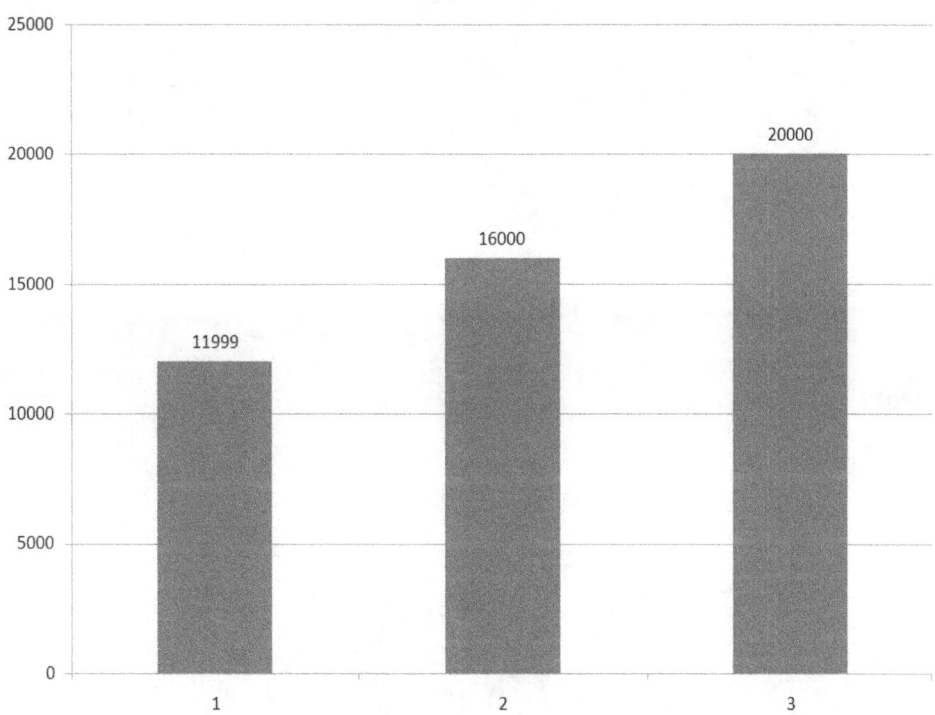

Domestic sales – 3 points

International sales – 1 point

Market Share 2011

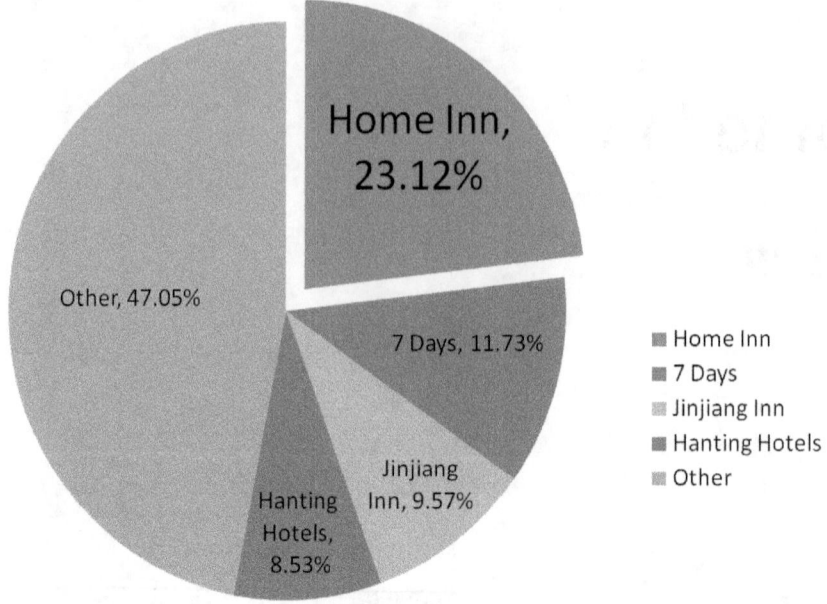

2012

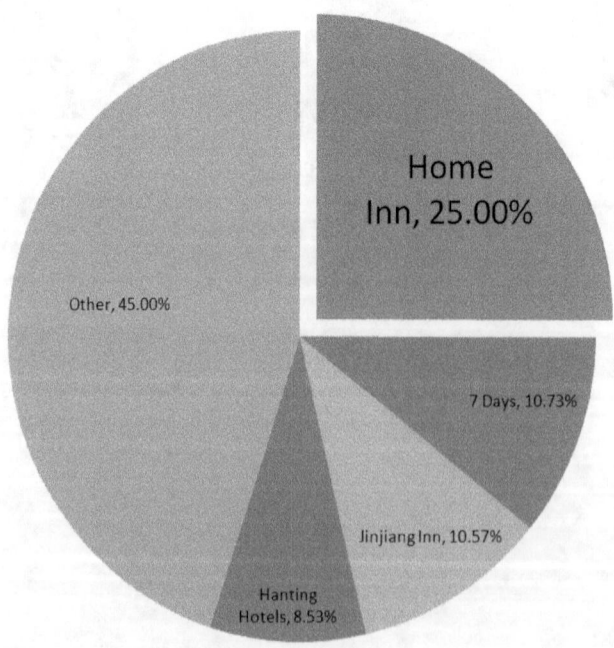

2013

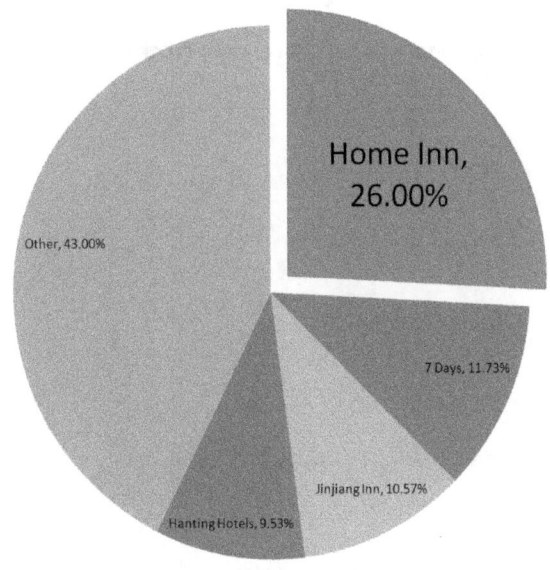

Domestic Market Share – 3 points

International Market Share – 1 point

Stock Price

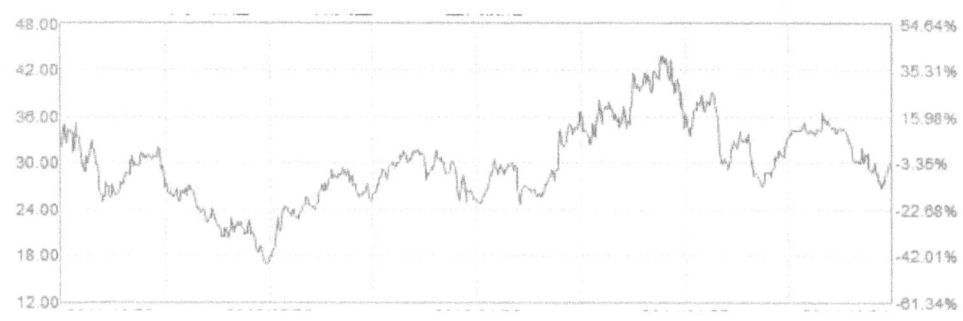

Stock Price – 0 points

Volatility – 3 points

Combined Total Score – 11pts-55%

Recommendation; Unacceptable; low international market share; poor stock performance

Hong Kong Savings Bank Sales

Domestic Sales – 1 point

International Sales – 1 point

Market Share 2011

销售额

- 1.2
- 1.4
- 3.2
- 8.2

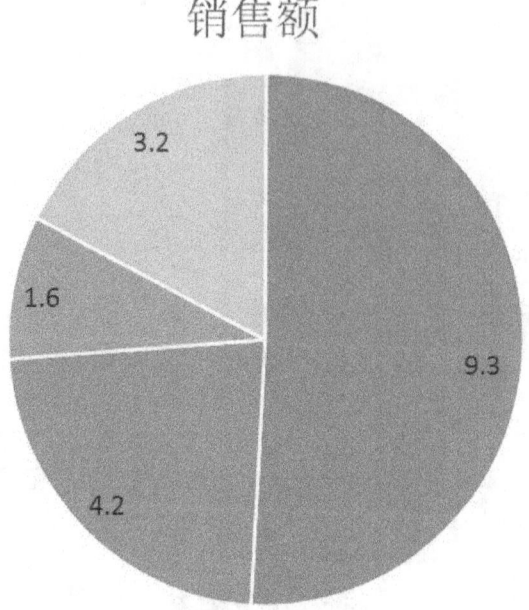

2013

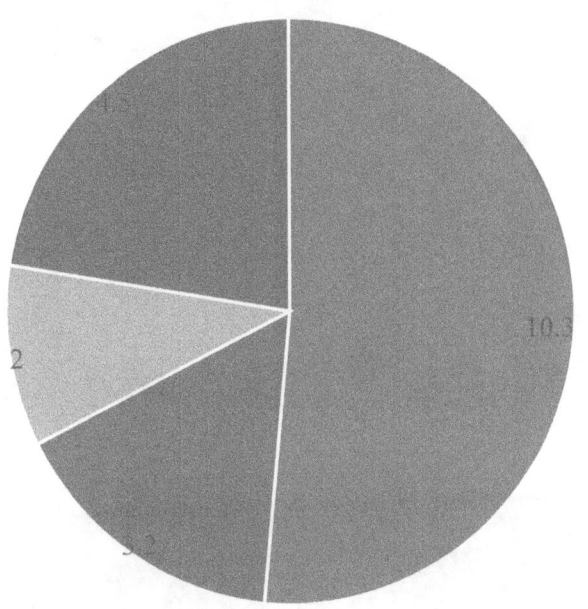

Domestic Market share – 1 point

International market share – 0 points

Stock Price

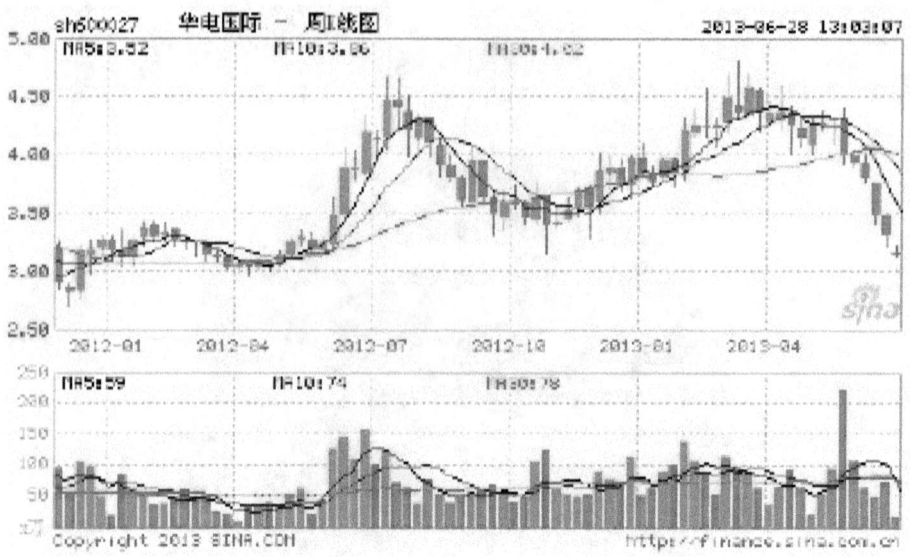

Stock price – 2 points

Volatility – 3 points

Total Combined Points – 8 points = 40%

Recommendation: unacceptable; no international market share, ok stock

Wahaha

Sales

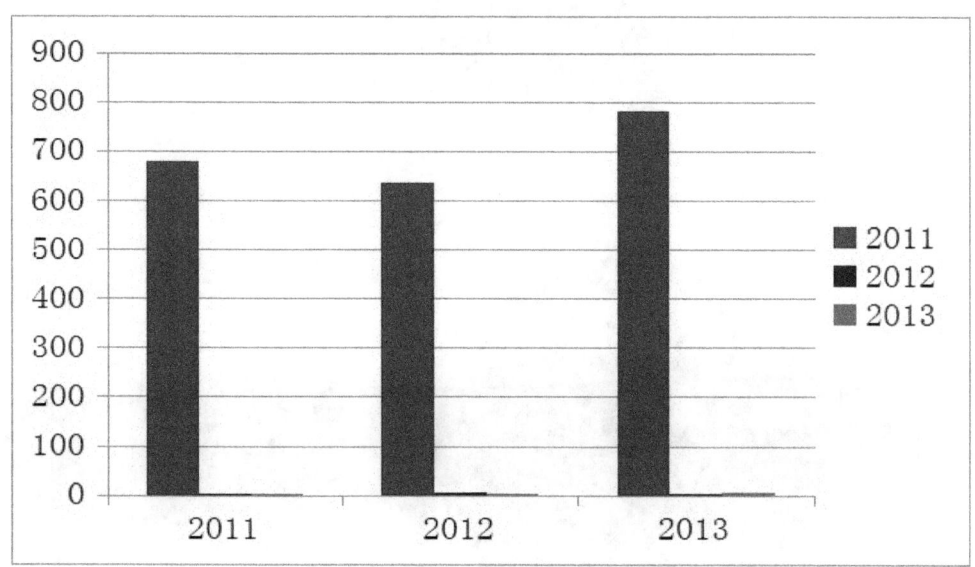

Domestic sales – 1 point

International sales – 0 points

Market share

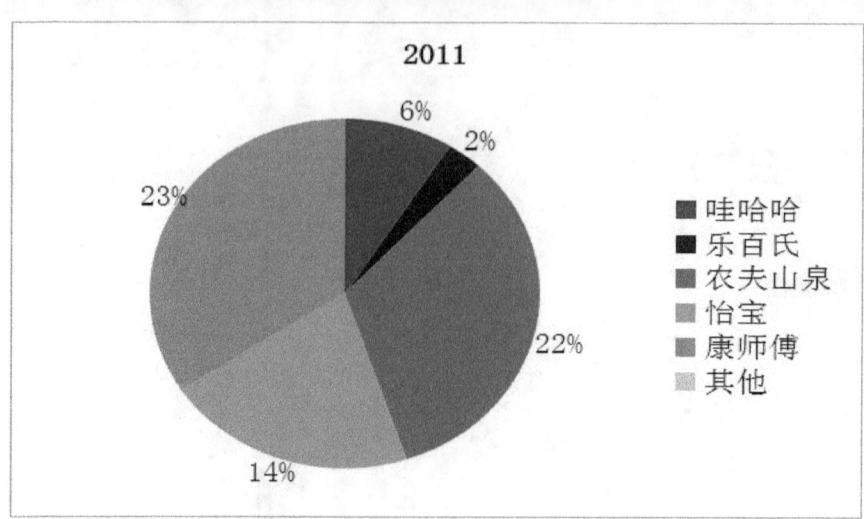

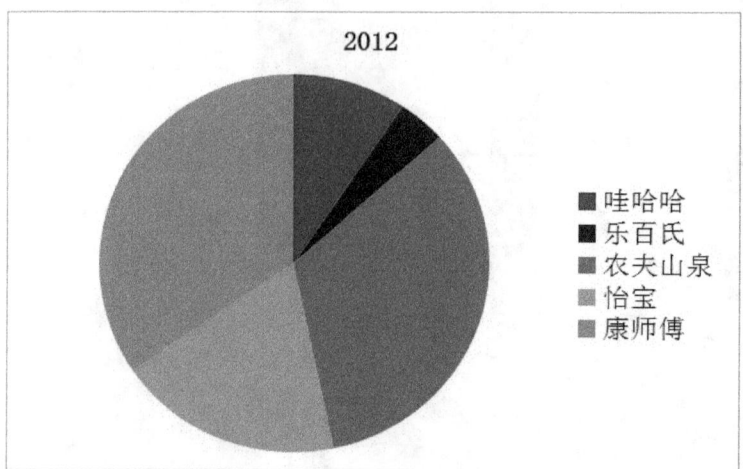

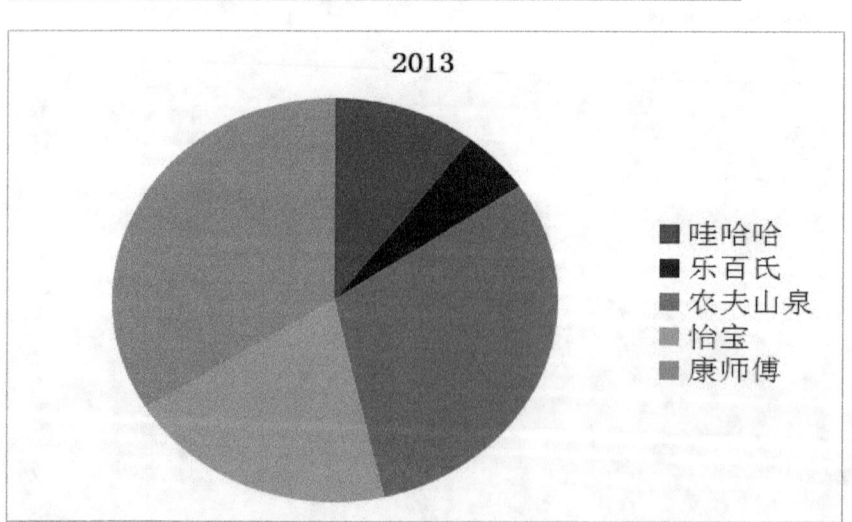

Domestic Market share – 1 point

International market share – 0 points

Stock price – no stock points

Total Combined Score – 2 points – 10%

Recommendation; unacceptable; no international market share; no stock

Huawei Sales

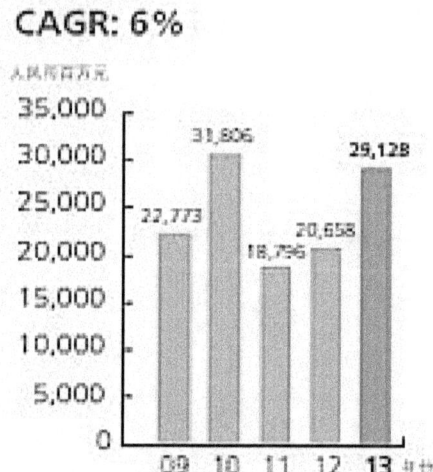

Domestic sales – 3 points

International sales – 2 points

Market share 2012

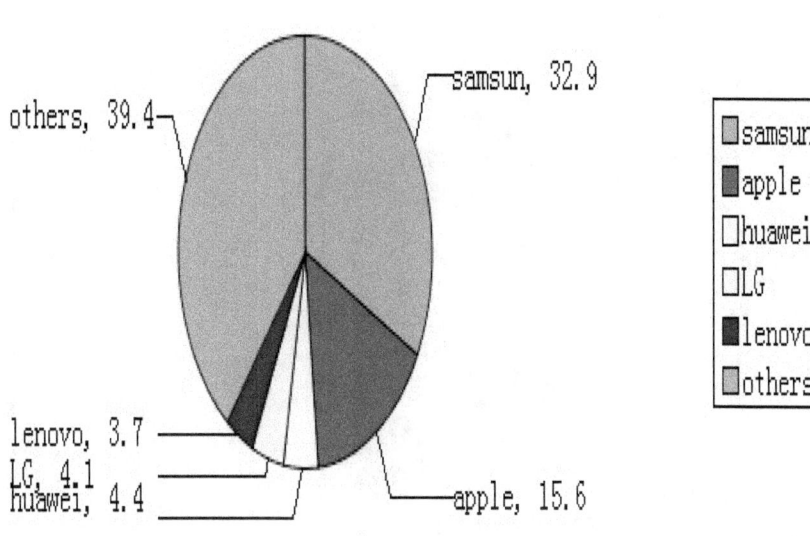

2013

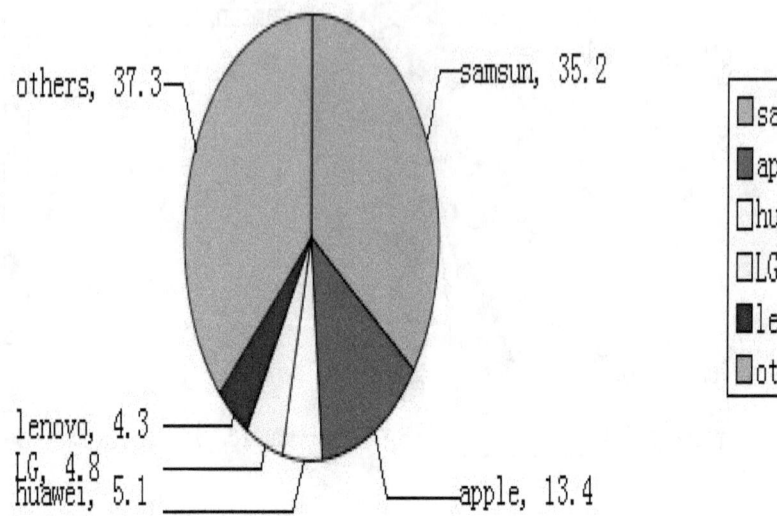

Domestic Market share points - 3 points

International Market share points – 2 points

Stock Price

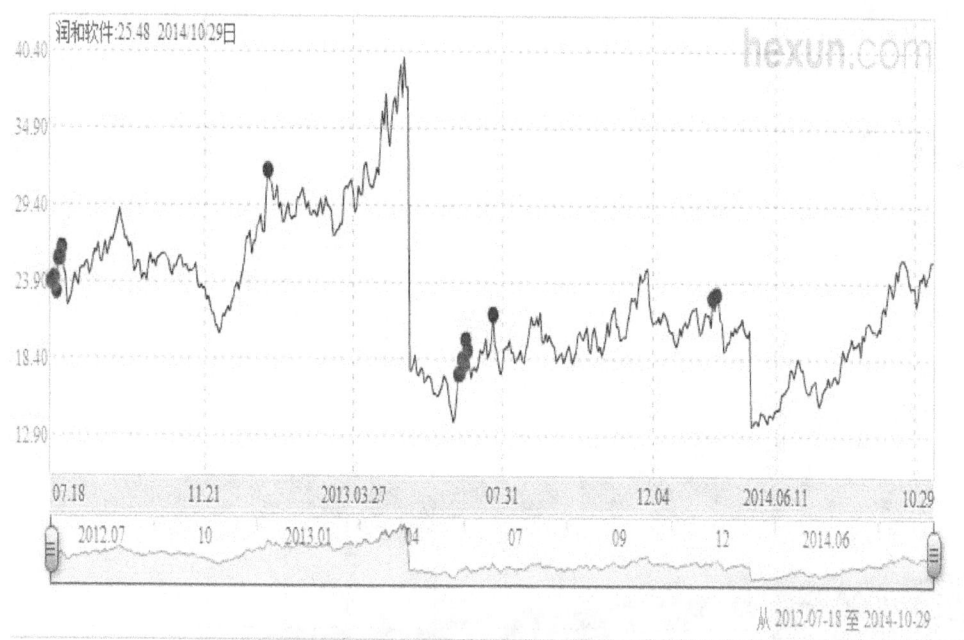

Stock price – 0 points

Volatility – 1 point

Total Combined Score – 11 pts=55%

Recommendation; unacceptable; poor stock performance with high volatility. Rejected in US

ICBC
Sales

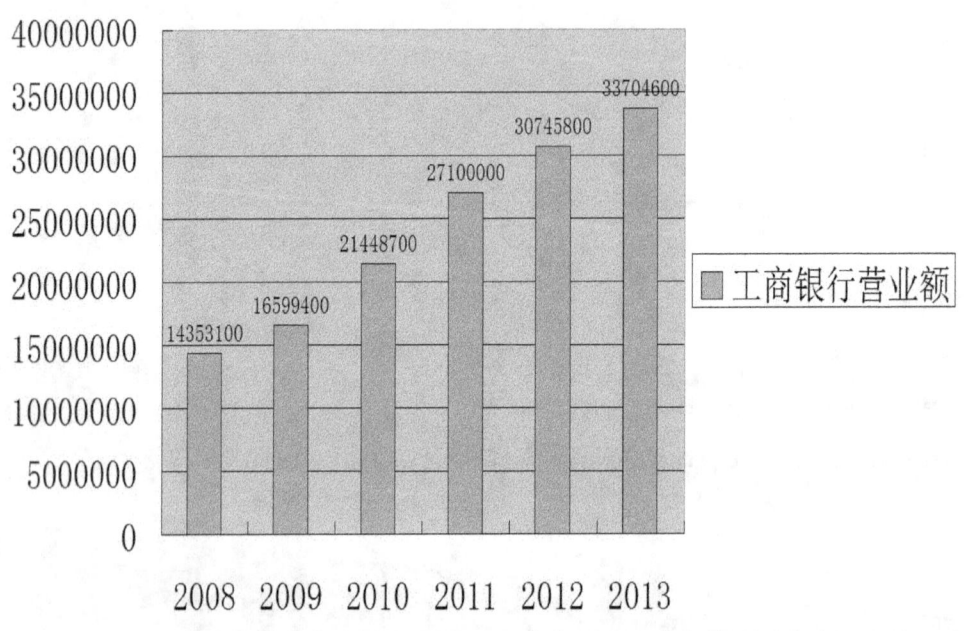

Domestic sales – 3 points

International sales – 0 points

Market Share 2012

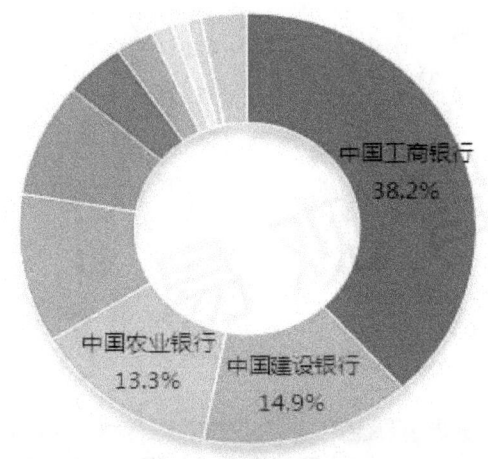

2013

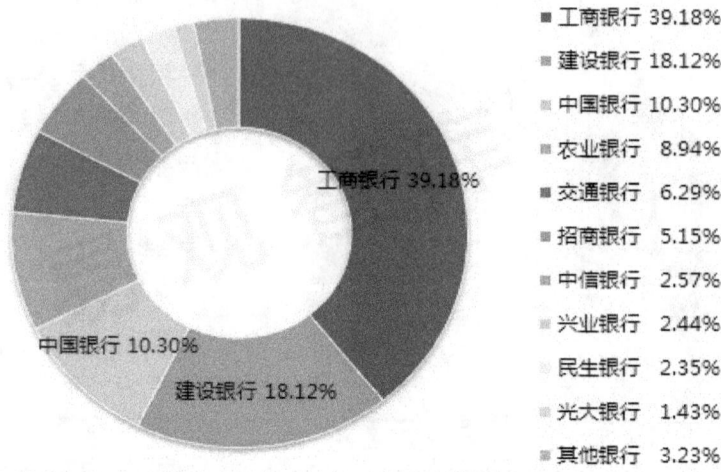

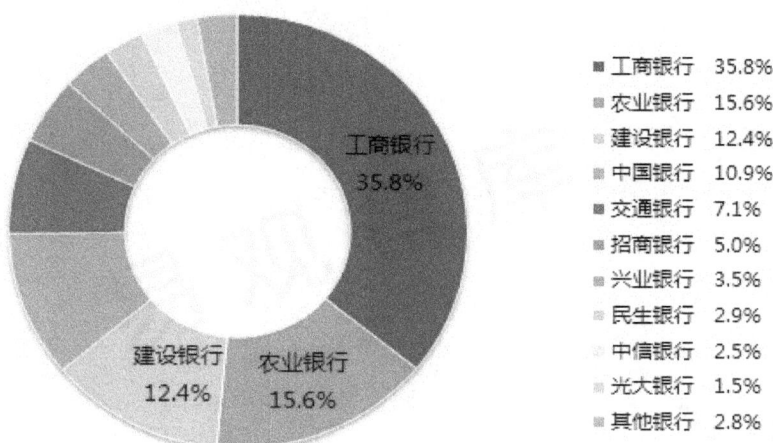

Domestic market share – 2 points

International market share - 0 points

Stock price

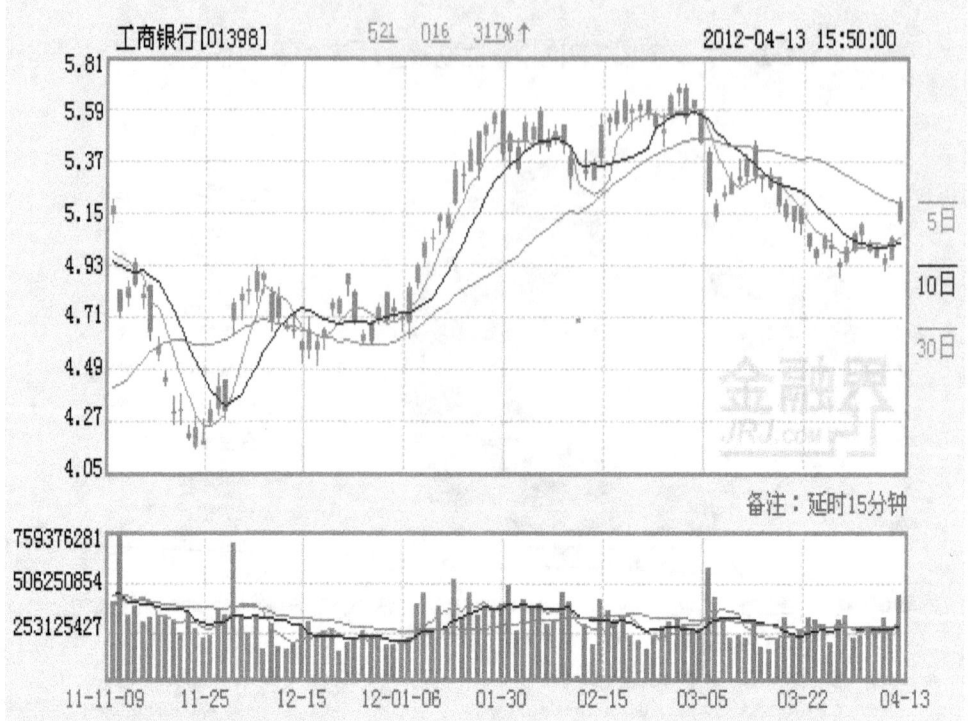

Stock price – 2 points

Volatility – 2 points

Total Combined Score – 9 points =45%

Recommendation: unacceptable; no international market share; stock ok

Jian Fa

Sales

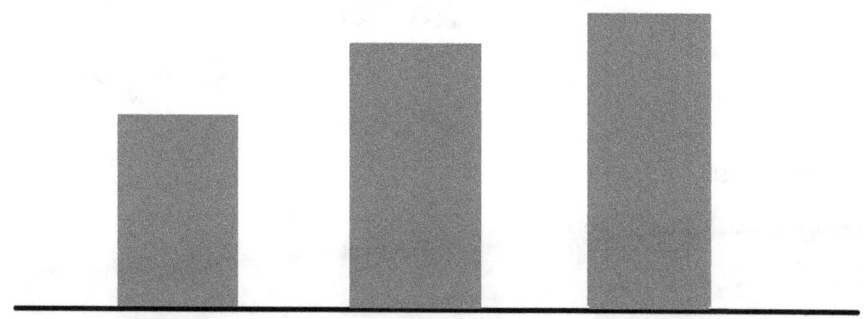

2011 2012 2013

Domestic sales – 3 points

International sales – 0 points

Market Share

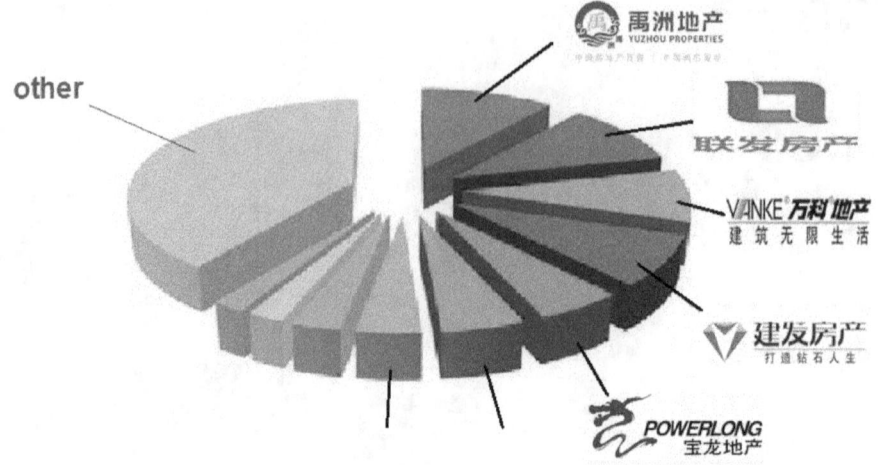

Domestic Market Share – 1 point

International Market Share – 0 points

Stock price

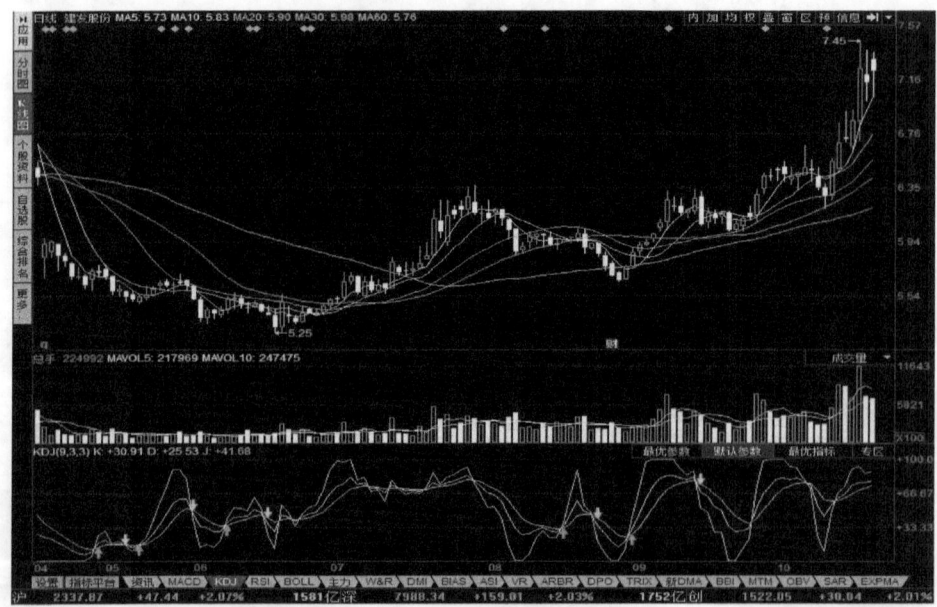

Stock price – 3 points

Volatility – 3 points

Total Combined Score – 10 points=50%

Recommendation; unacceptable : no international market share, but good domestic results for stock

Lenovo Sales

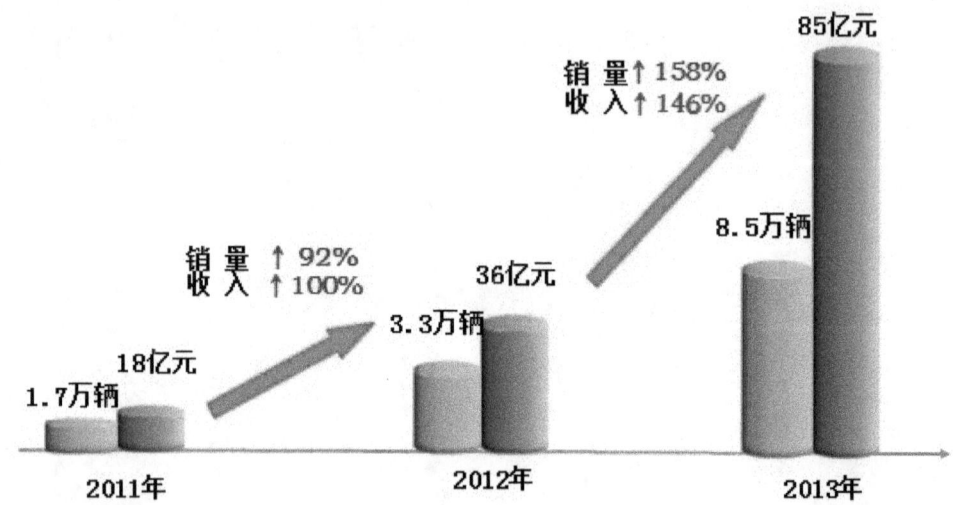

Domestic sales – 3 points

International Sales – 3 points

Market Share

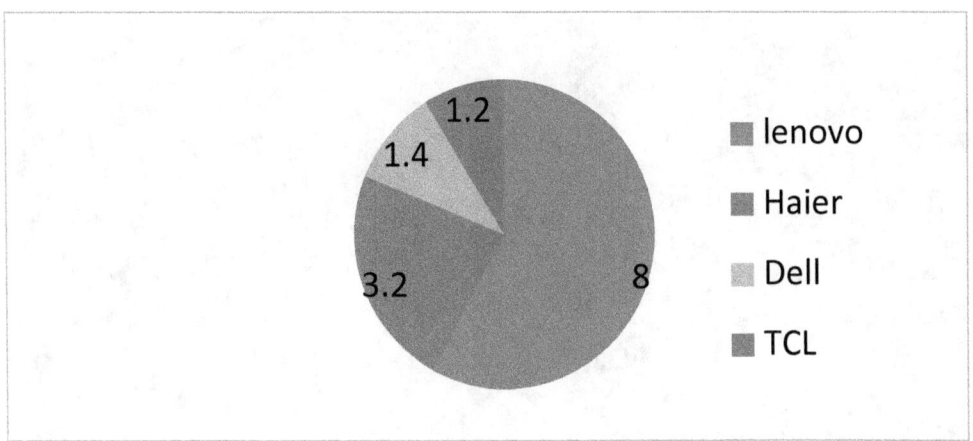

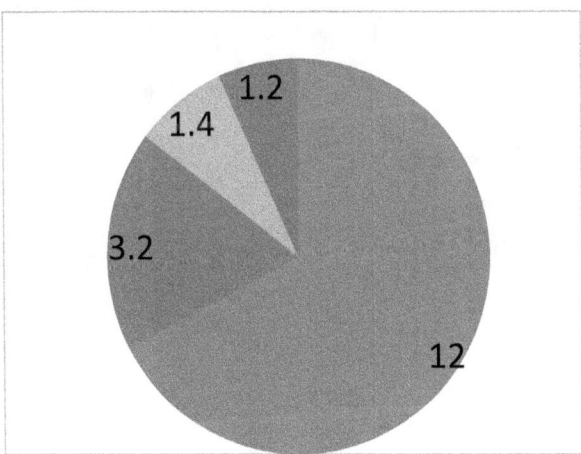

Domestic Market Share – 3 points

International Market Share – 3 points

Stock Price

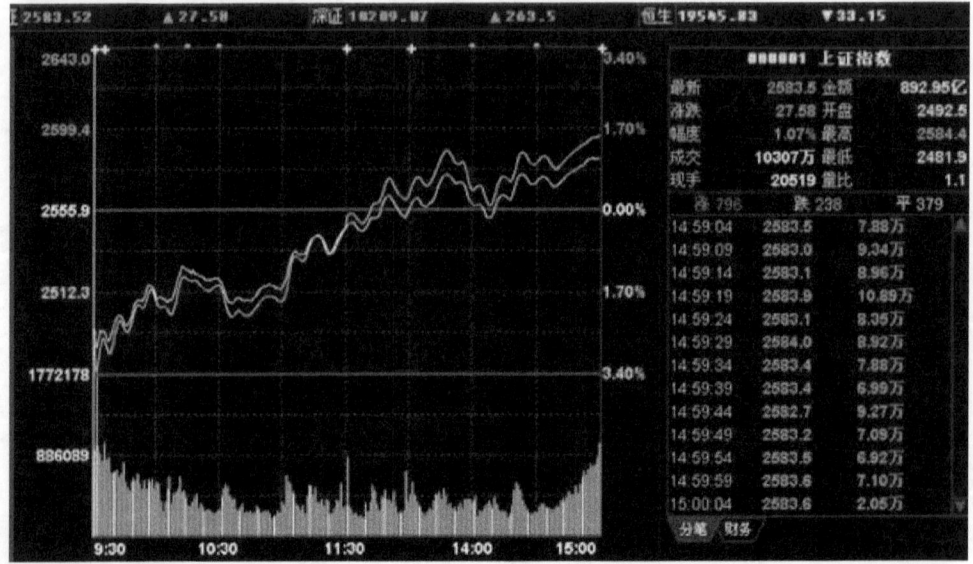

Stock price – 3 points

Volatility – 3 points

Total Combined Score – 18 points=90%

Recommendation: Strong Buy; one of the best Chinese stocks

Li-Ning
Sales

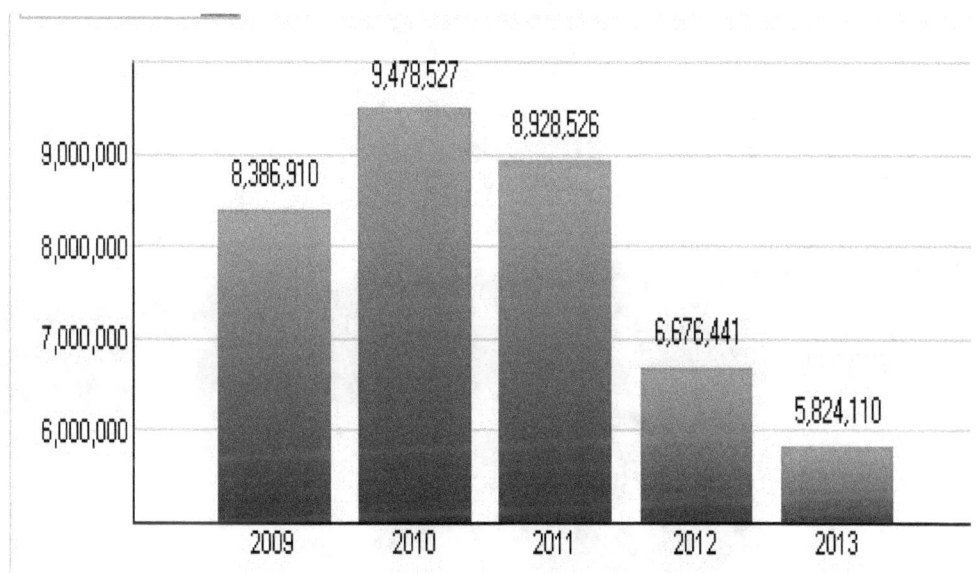

Domestic sales – 0 points

International Sales – 0 points

Market Share

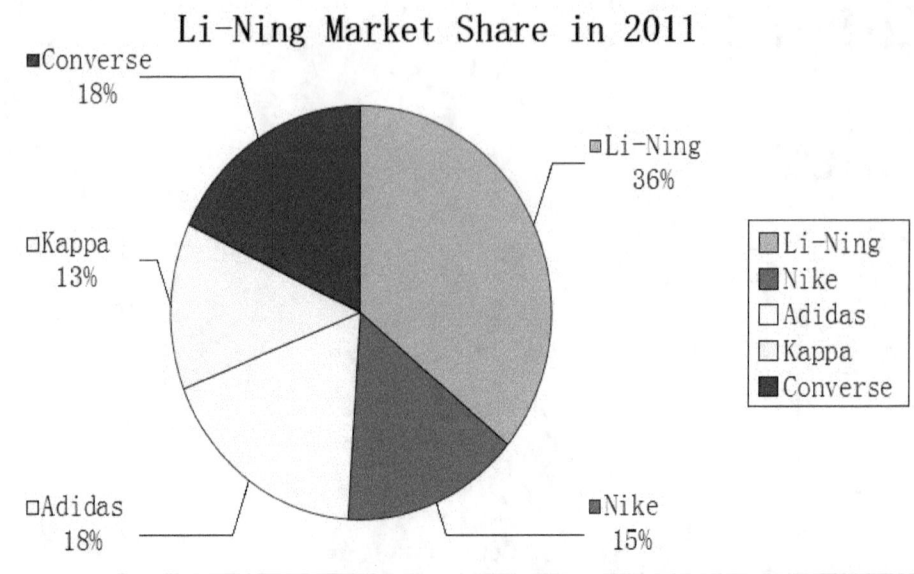

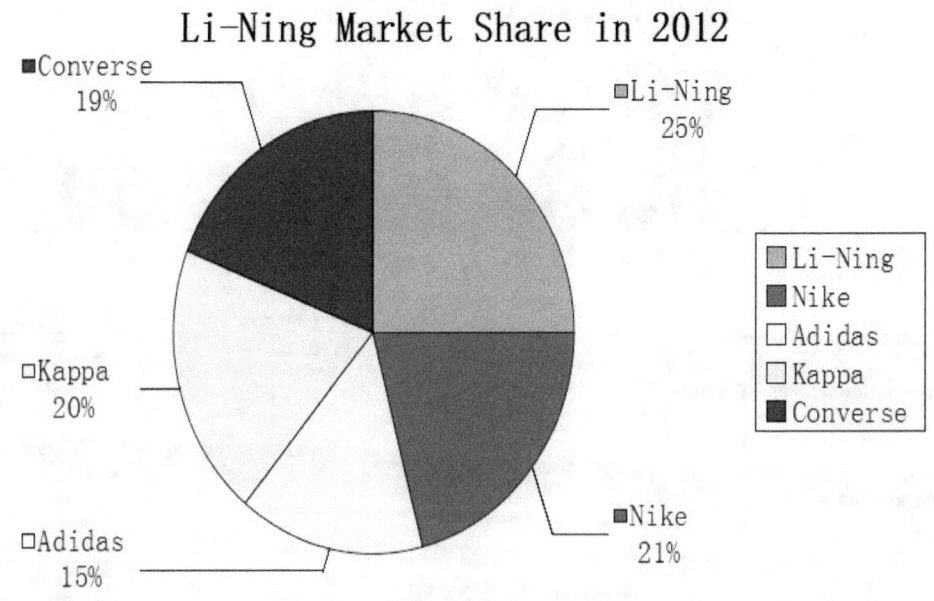

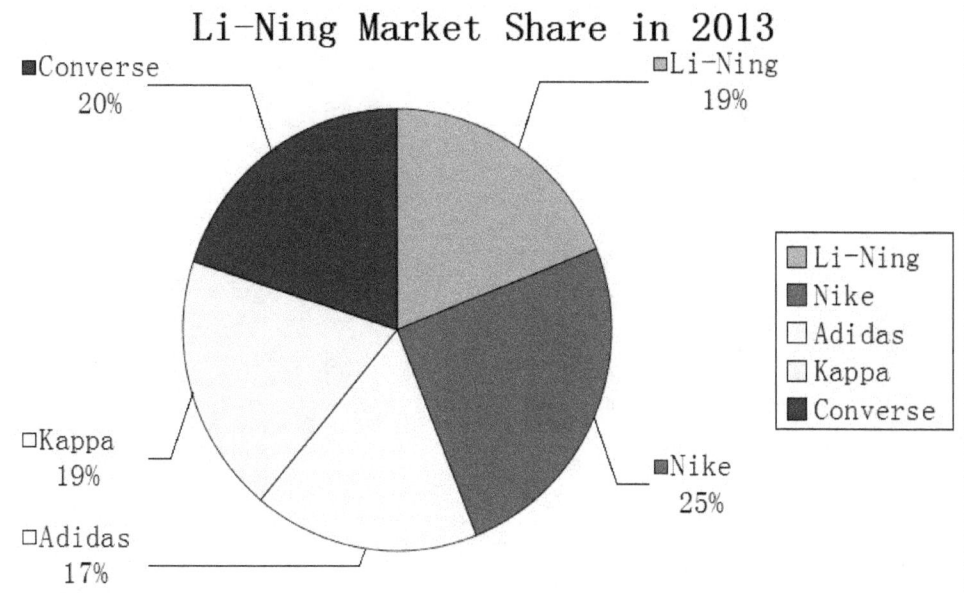

Domestic market share – 0 points

International Market share – 0 points

Stock Price

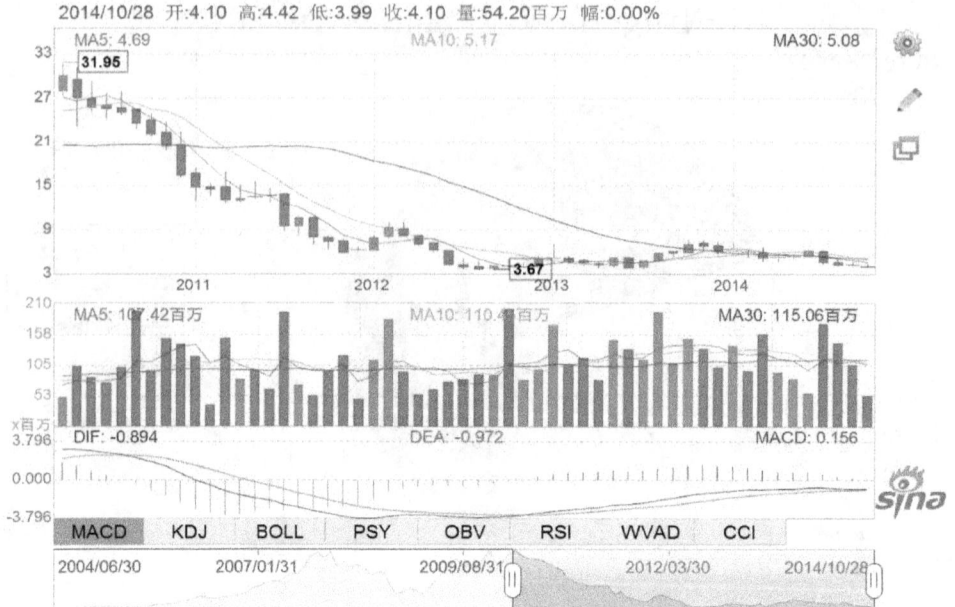

Stock price – 0 points

Volatility – 1 point

Total Combined Score – 1 point – 5%

Recommendation: You have a better chance of winning the Kentucky Derby with a 20-1 shot than making money with this turkey. One of the worst stocks in China and getting eaten alive in market share.

Meizu Sales

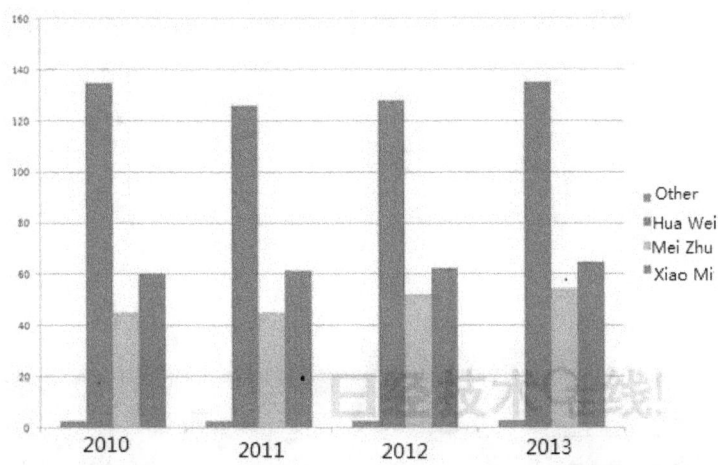

Domestic Sales – 1 point

International Sales – 0 points

Market Share 2012

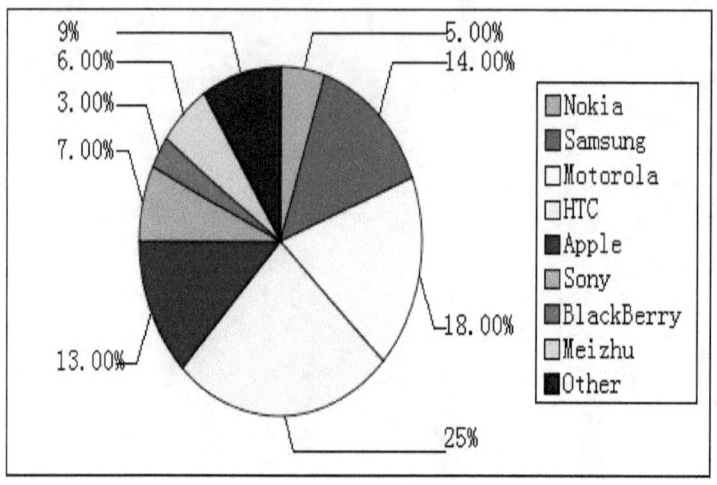

2013

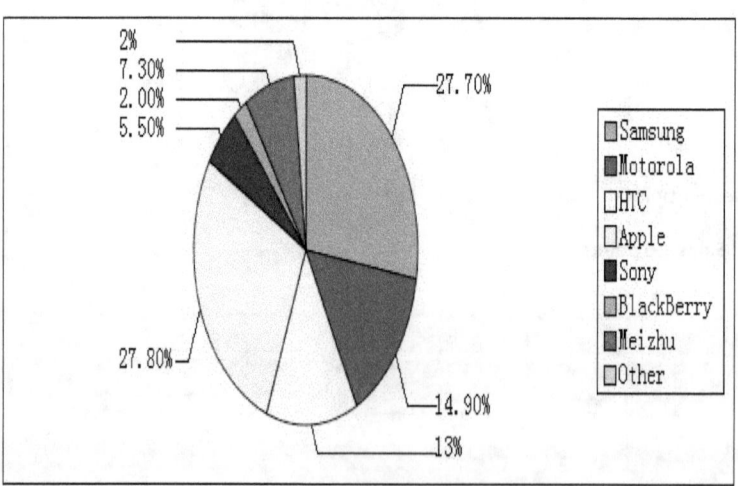

2014

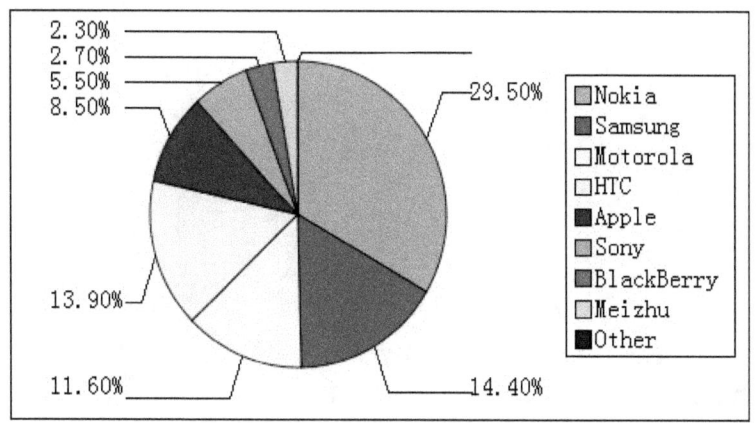

Domestic market share – 0 points

International market share – 0 points

Stock Price

Stock price – 1 point

Volatility – 3 points

Total Combined Score – 5 points=25%

Recommendation: unacceptable; market share sinking faster than the Titanic; no international market share

Mengniu

Sales

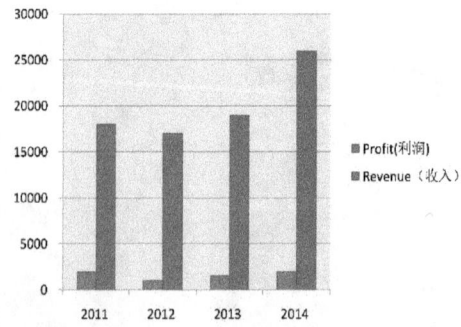

Domestic sales – 1 point
International sales – 0 points

Market Share

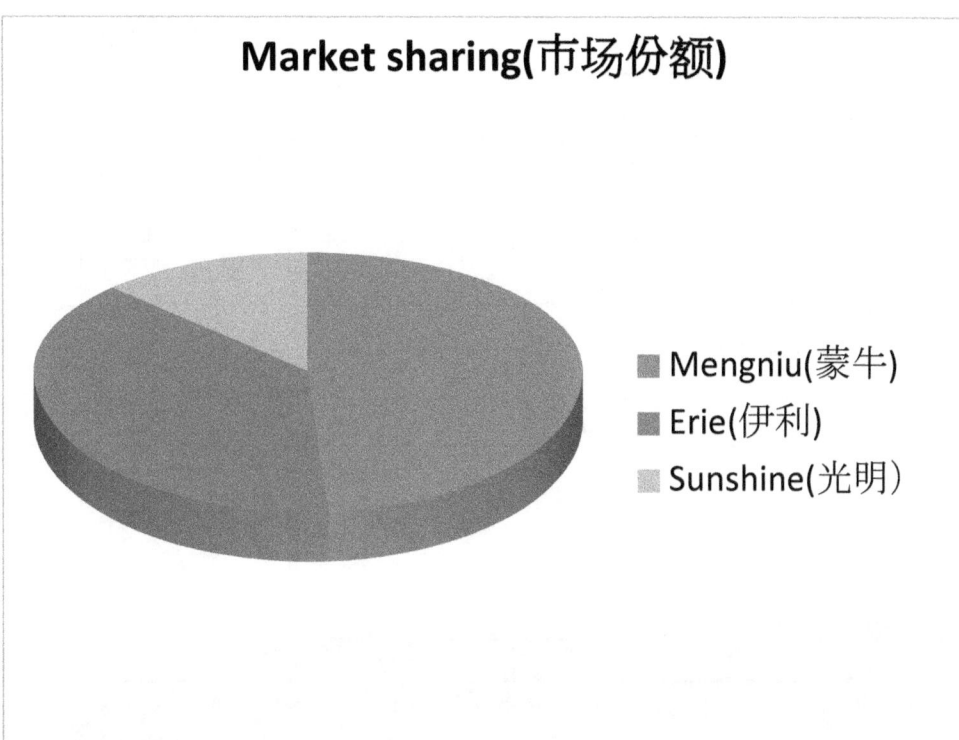

Domestic market share – 1 point

International market share – 0 points

Stock Price

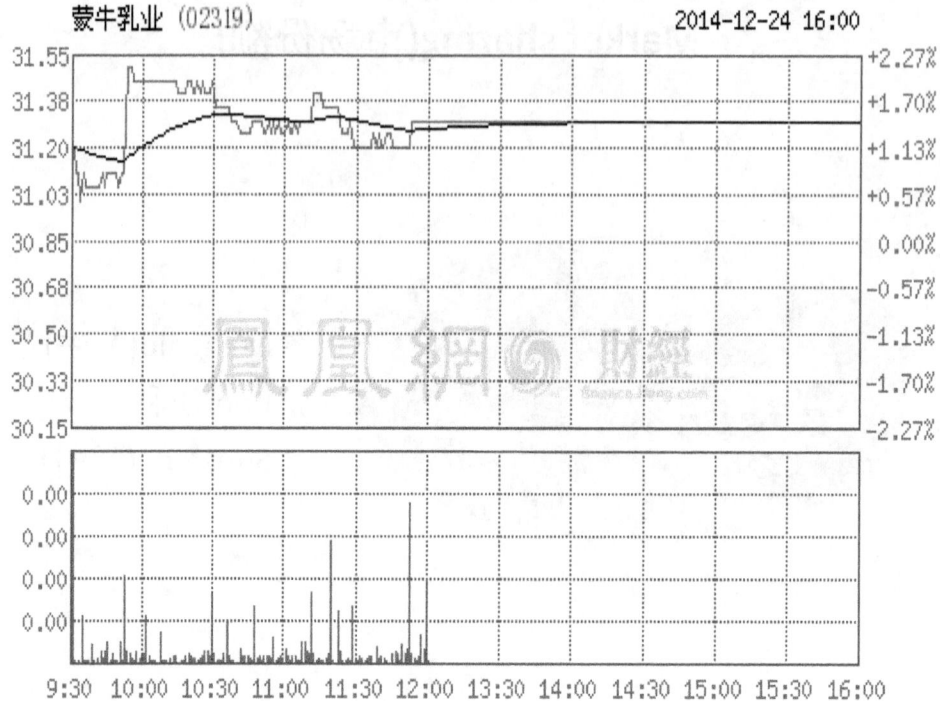

Stock price – 0 points

Volatility – 3 points

Total Combined Score – 5 points – 25%

Recommendation – Unacceptable – There are coma patients with more of a pulse than this company's stock. No international market share.

Midea
Sales

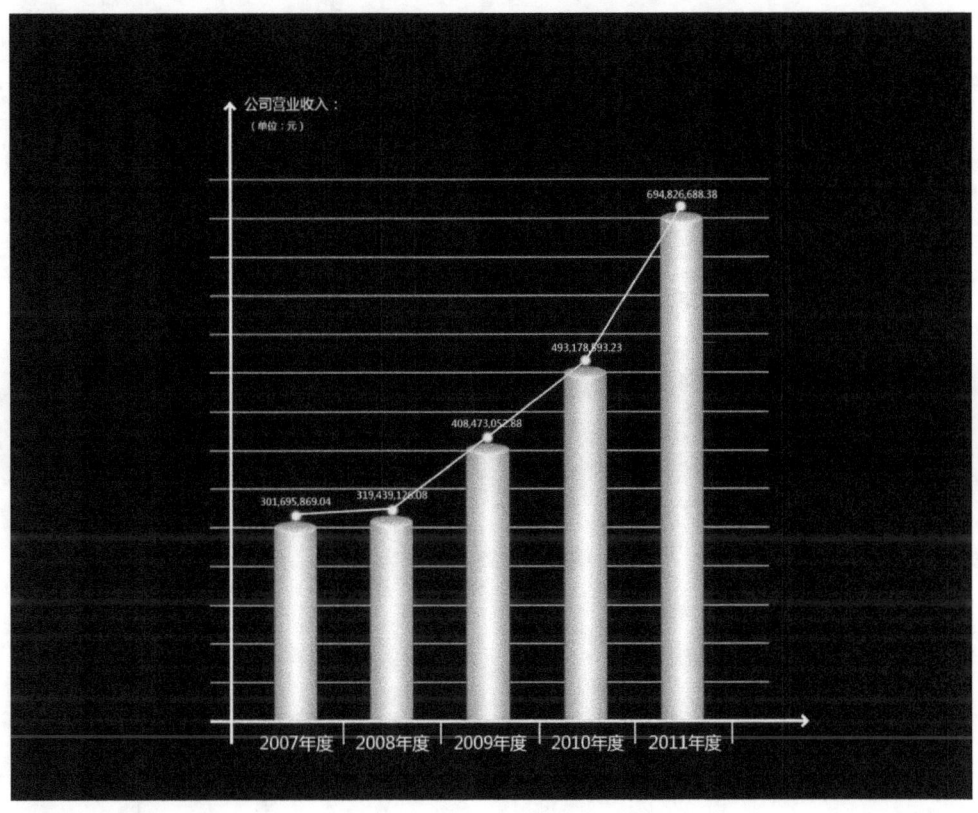

Domestic sales – 3 points

International Sales – 0 points

Market Share 2009

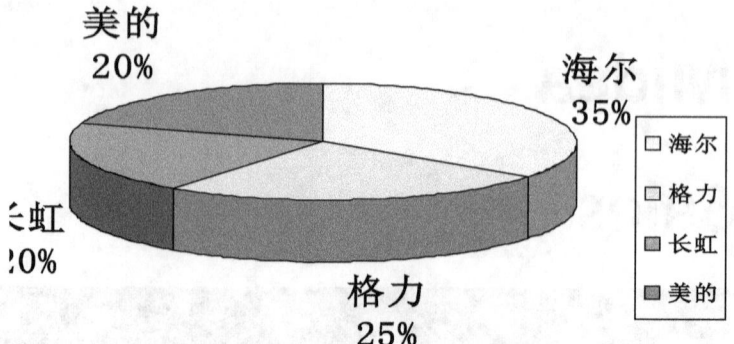

2010

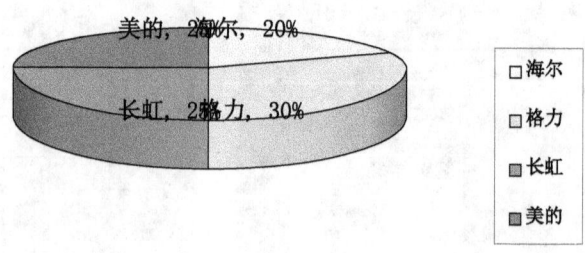

2011

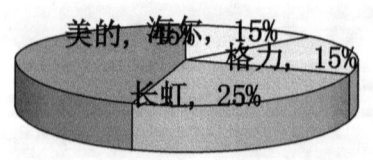

Domestic market share – 3 points

International market share – 0 points

Stock Price

Stock price – 3 points

Volatility – 3 points

Total Combined Score – 12 points=60pts

Recommendation: Guarded Buy: no international market share, but good domestic numbers and stock performance.

Muji

Sales

	2011	2012	2013
MUJI	165	150	170
IKAE	140	144	130

Domestic sales – 1 point

International Sales – 1 point

Market Share

2011

\

	2011			2012			2013
MUJI	35		MUJI	38		MUJI	42
IKEA	21		IKEA	22		IKEA	25
OTHERS	44		OTHERS	40		OTHERS	33

2012

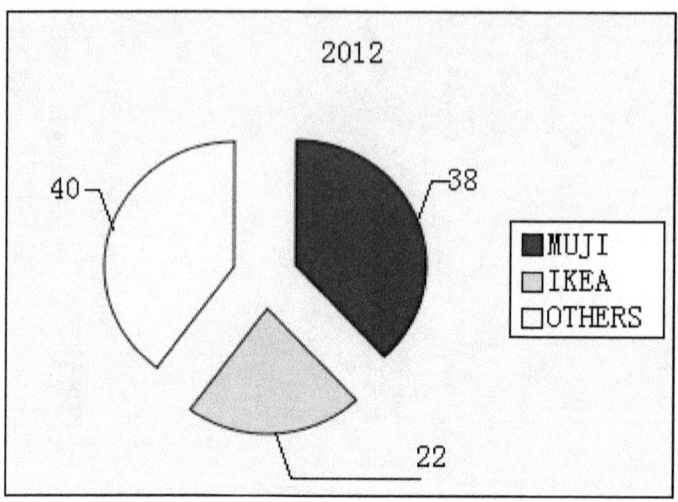

2013

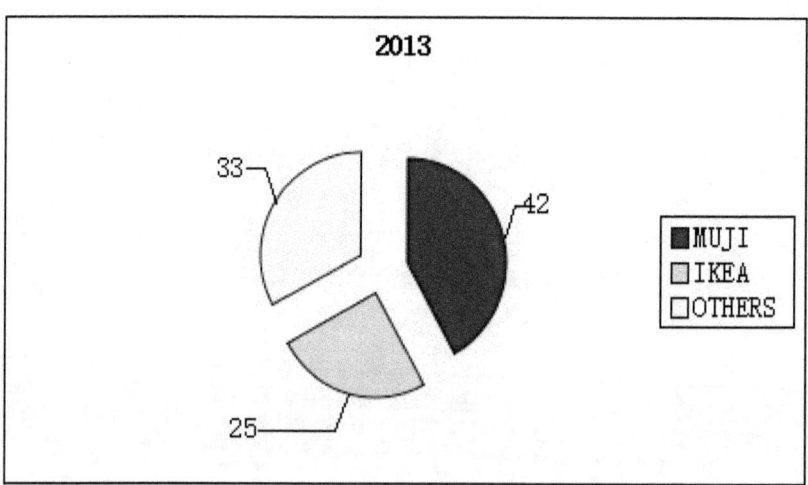

Domestic Market Share – 2 points

International Market Share – 2 points

Stock Price

	1	2	3	4	5	6	7	8	9	10	11	12
2011	22	24	31	35	29	38	26	36	34	22	27	39
2012	25	26	28	31	33	33	32	34	33	36	35	35
2013	32	29										35

Stock Price - 0 points

Volatility – 3 points

Total Combined Score – 9 points = 45%

Recommendation – Unacceptable – good international market share, but weak domestic sales and stock performance.

QQ Sales

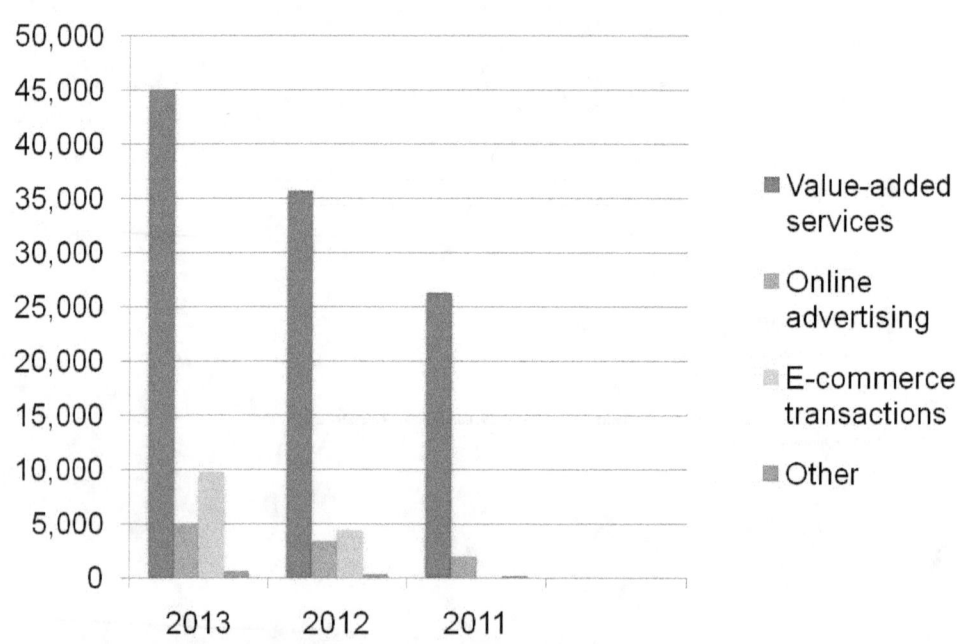

Domestic Sales – 3 points

International Sales – 0 points

Market Share

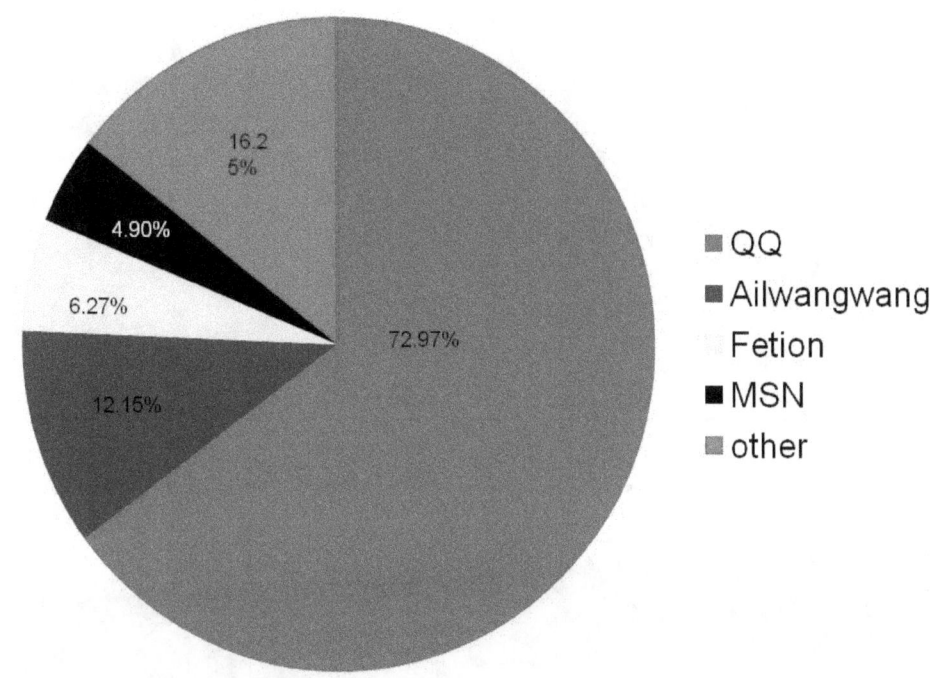

Domestic Market share - 3 points

International Market Share – 0 points

Stock Price

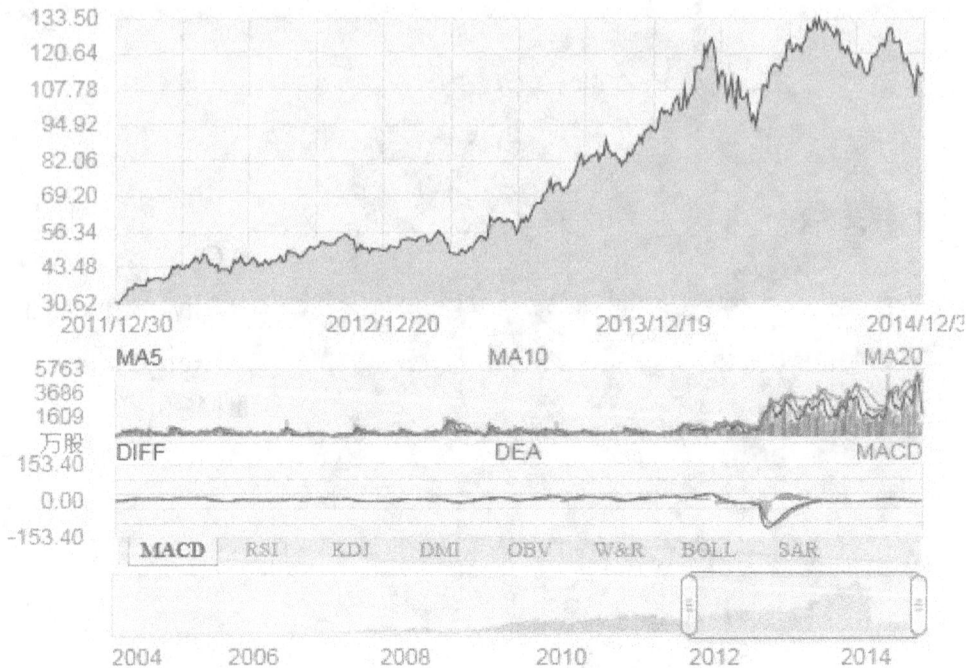

Stock price – 3 points

Volatility – 3 points

Total Combined Score – 12 points – 60%

Recommendation: Guarded Buy; great domestic numbers and stock performance, but dismal international market share

Sina

Sales

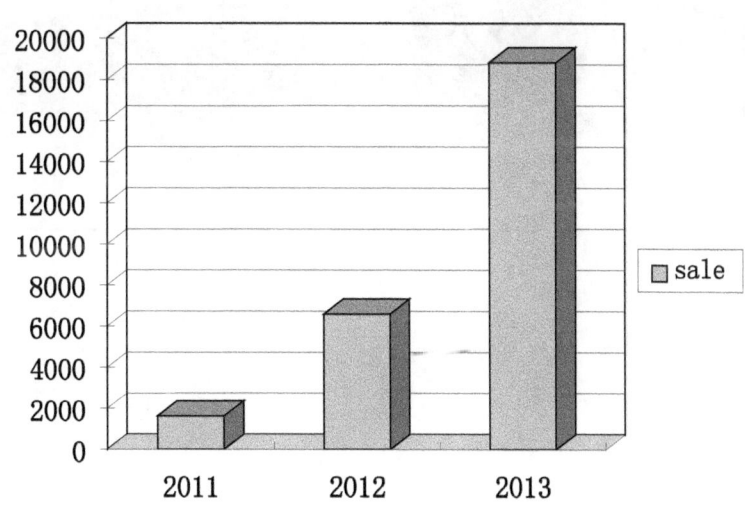

Domestic Sales – 3 points

International Sales – 0 points

Market Share

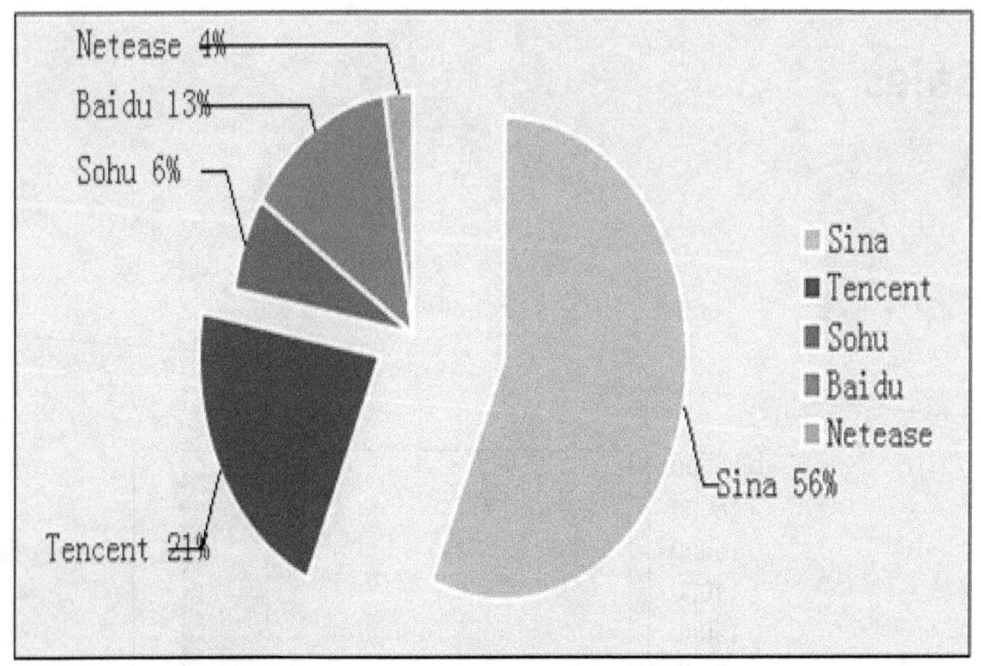

2012

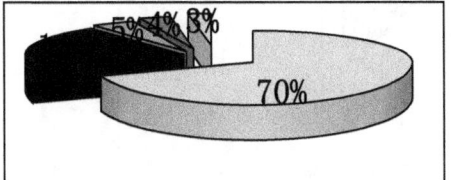

2013

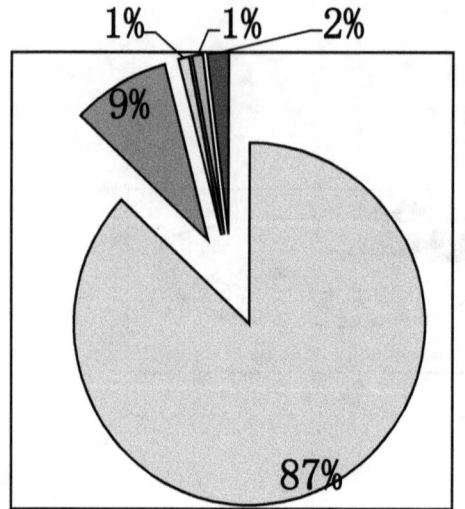

Domestic Market Share – 3 points

International Market Share – 0 points

Stock Price

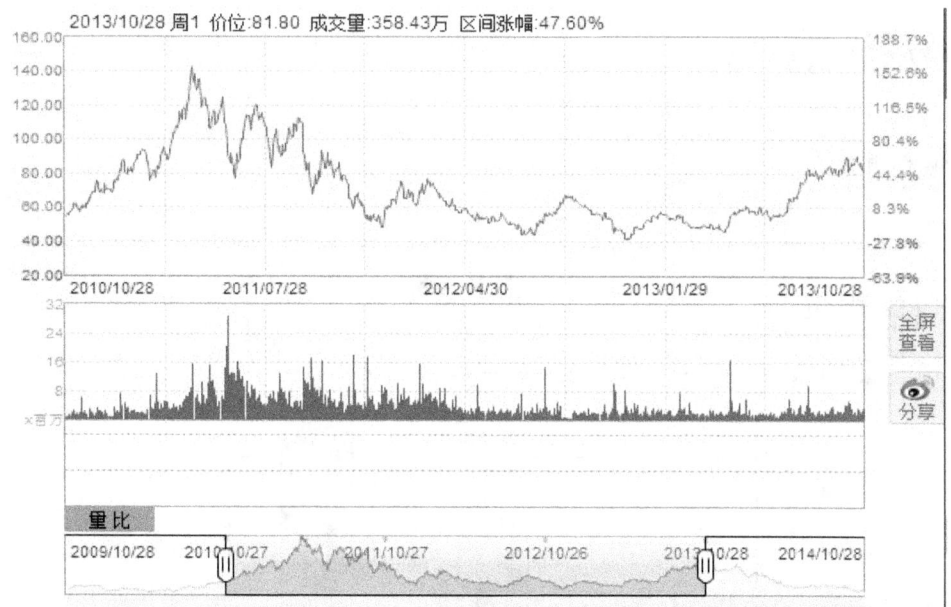

Stock price – 1 point

Volatility – 2 points

Total Combined Score – 9 points – 45%

Recommendation – Unacceptable – stock performance does not match domestic market share claims; no international market share

Sinopec Sales

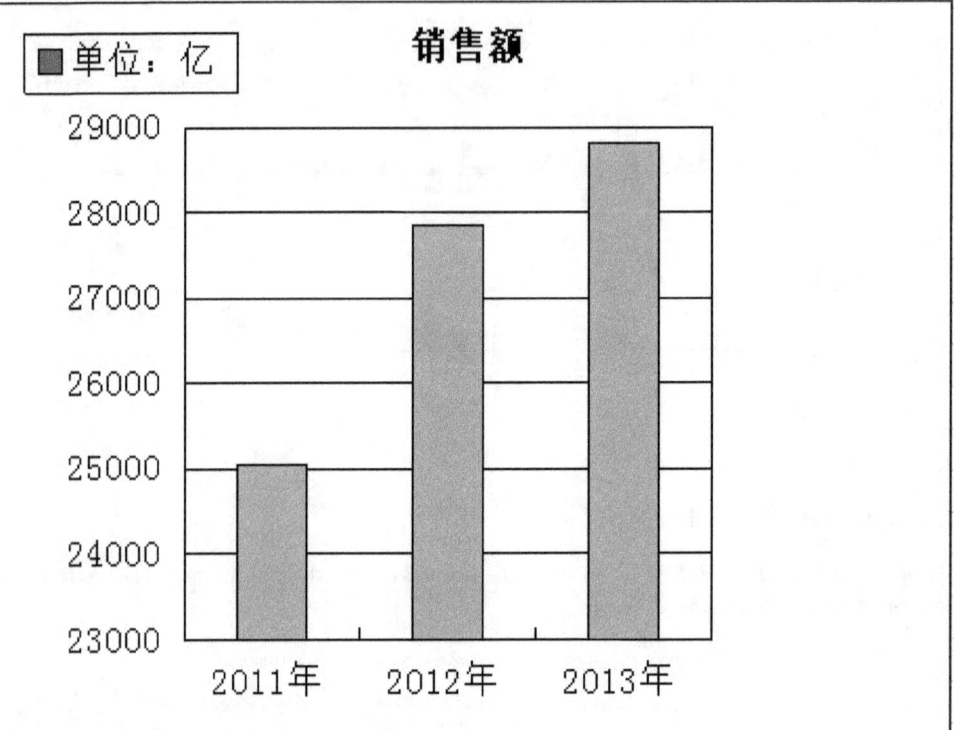

Domestic Sales – 3 points

International Sales – 1 point

Market Share (dark blue)

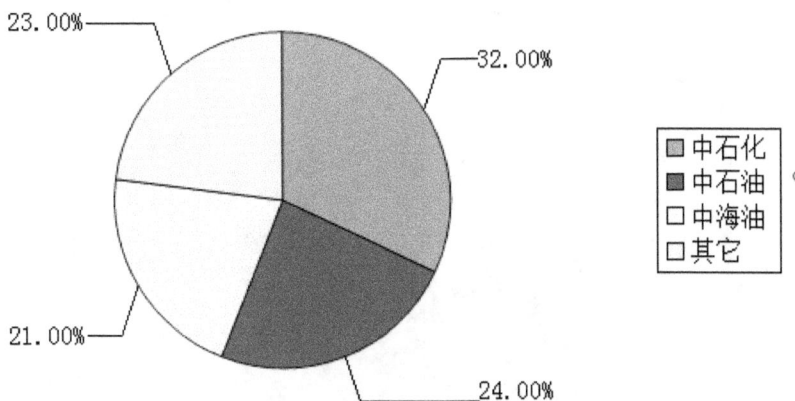

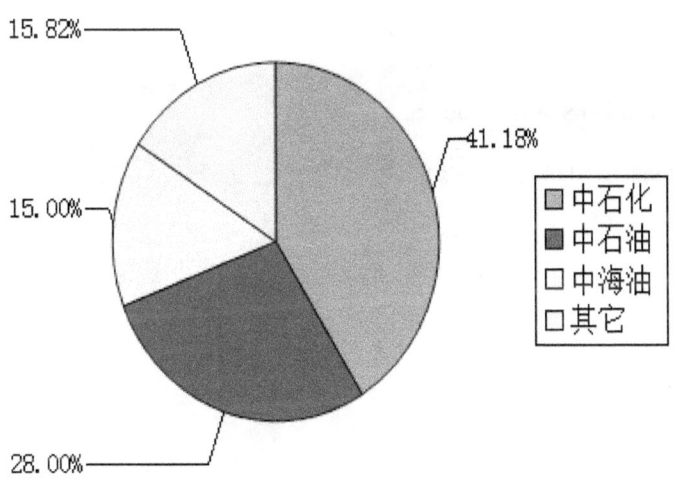

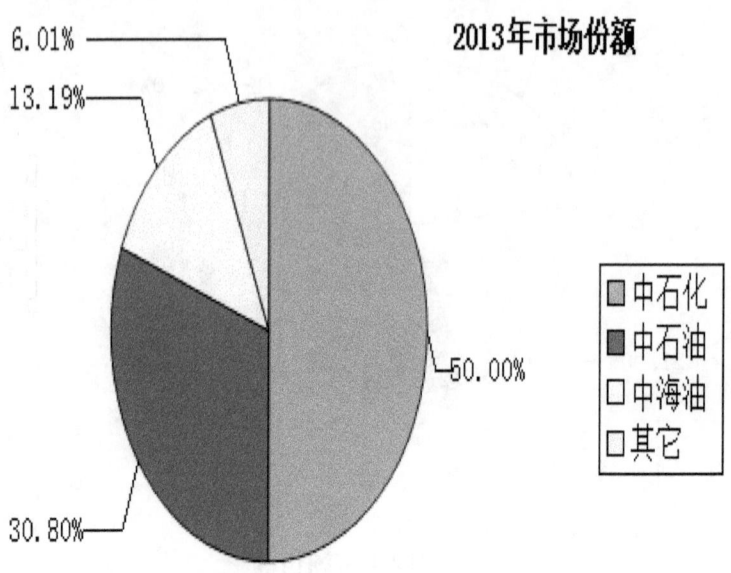

Domestic Market Share – 3 points

International Market Share – 1 point

Stock Price

Stock price – 0 points

Volatility – 3 points

Total Combined Score – 11 points – 55%

Recommendation – Unacceptable – poor stock performance and weak international market share

Taobao Sales

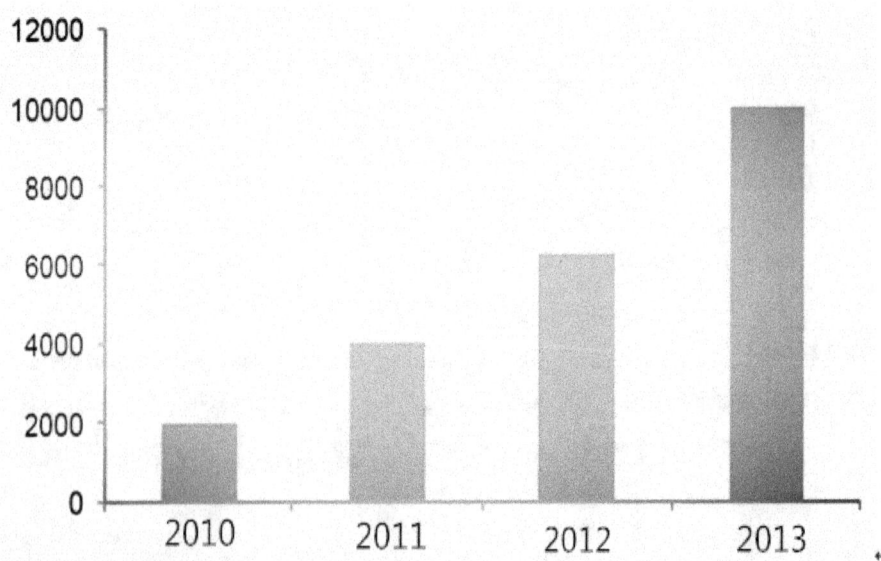

Domestic Sales – 3 points

International Sales – 2 points

Market Share

2011

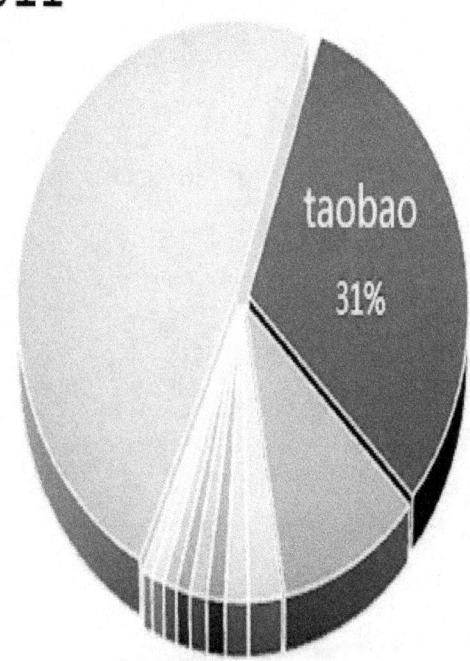

- taobao
- 京东商城 10.2%
- 卓越亚马逊 2.3%
- 当当 1.6%
- newegg 1.3%
- VANCL 1.2%
- 苏宁易购 1.0%
- M18 0.9%
- 易迅 0.8%
- 库巴网 0.7%
- 其他 48.6%

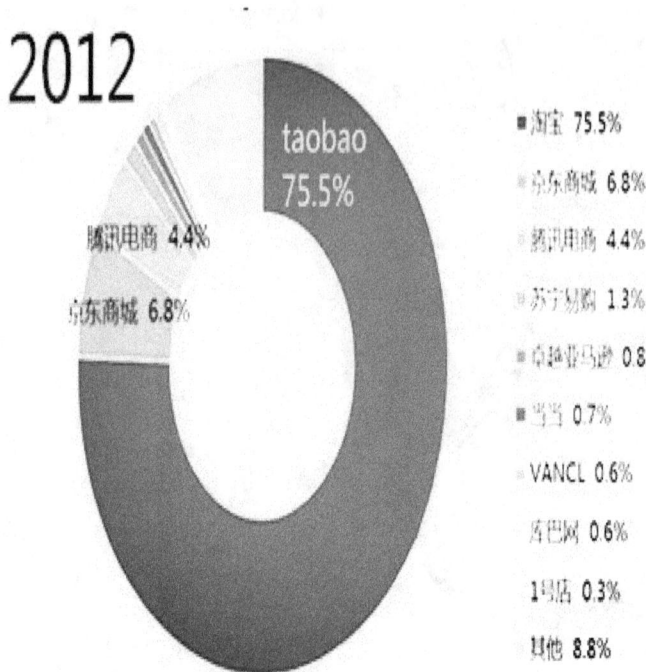

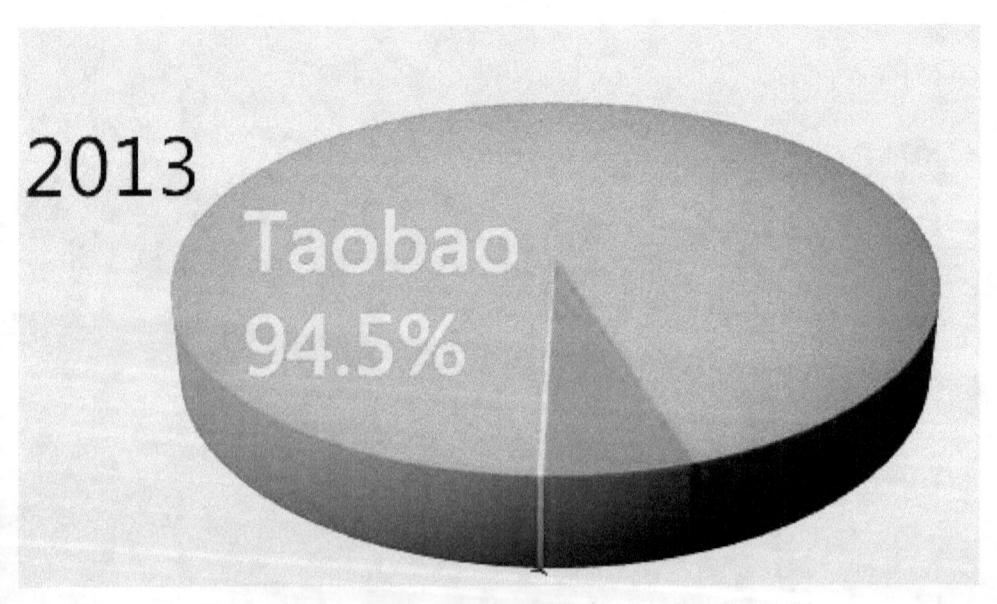

Domestic Market Share – 3 points

International Market Share – 2 points

Stock Price

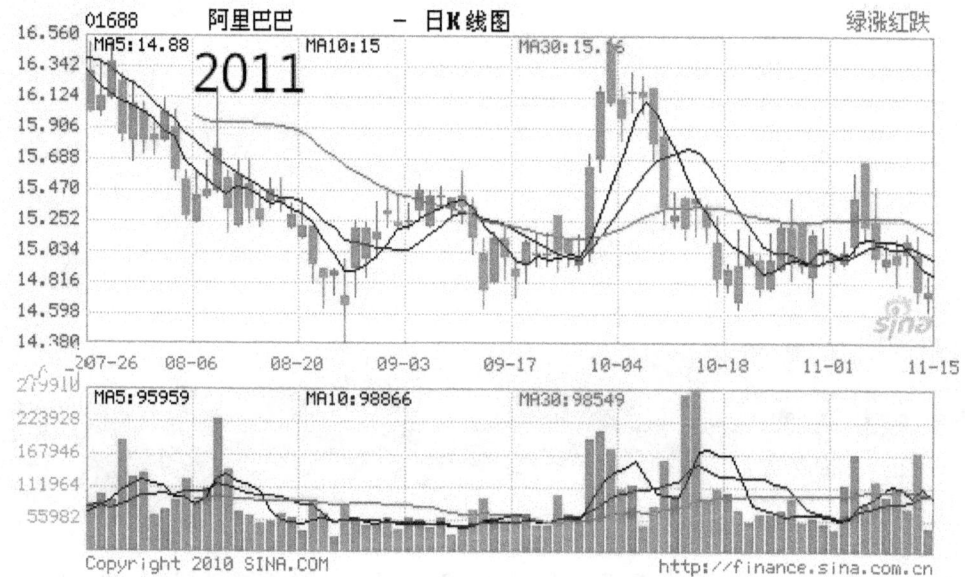

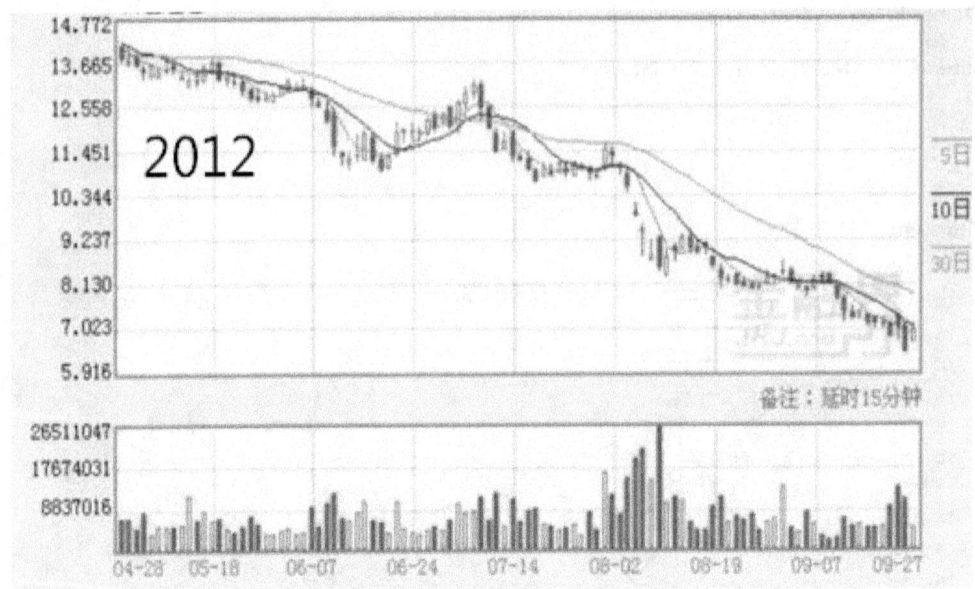

Stock price – 0 points

Volatility – 1 point

Total Combined Score – 11 points – 55%

Recommendation: unacceptable; poor stock performance despite good domestic and international numbers.

Wanda
Sales

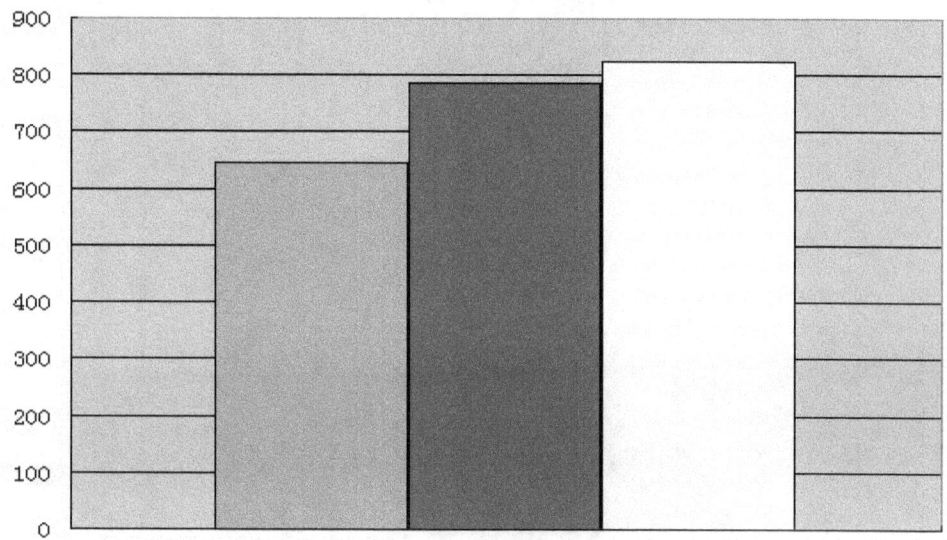

Domestic Sales – 3 points

International Sales – 1 point

Market Share 2011

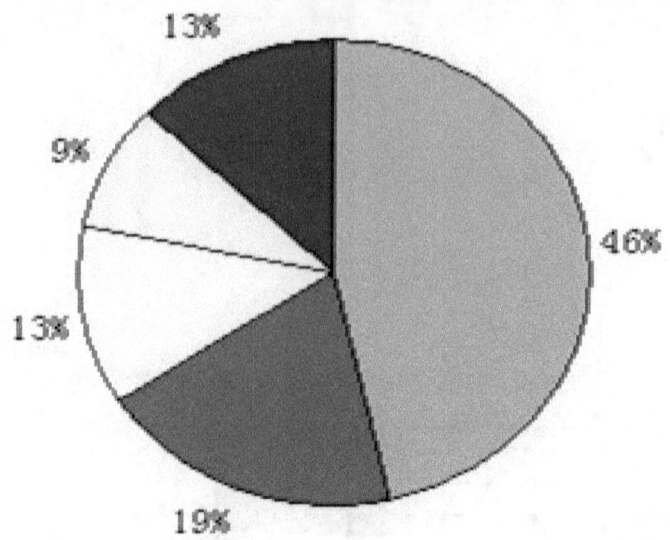

2012

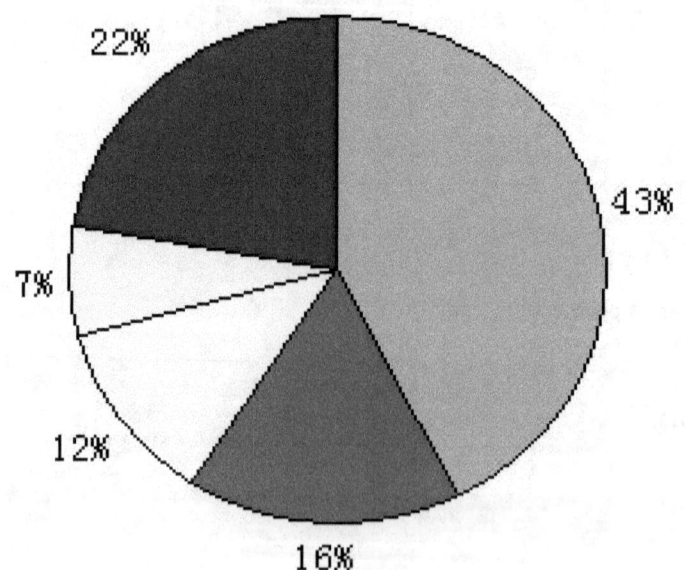

2013

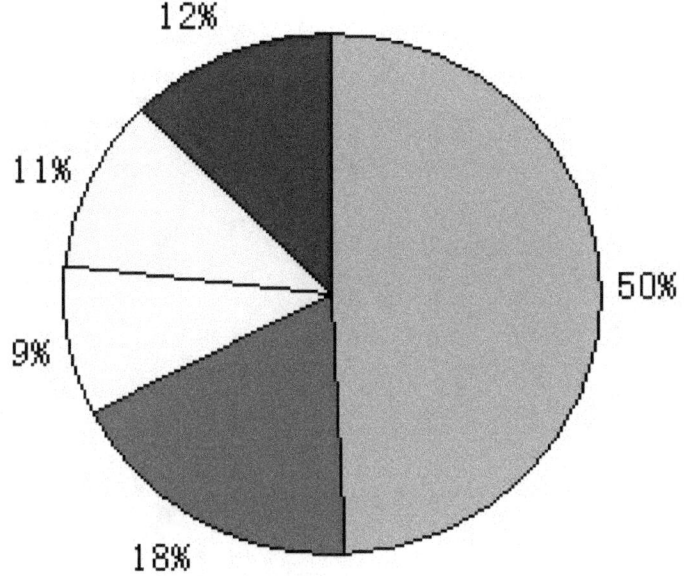

Domestic Market Share – 2 points

International Market Share – 1 point

Stock Price

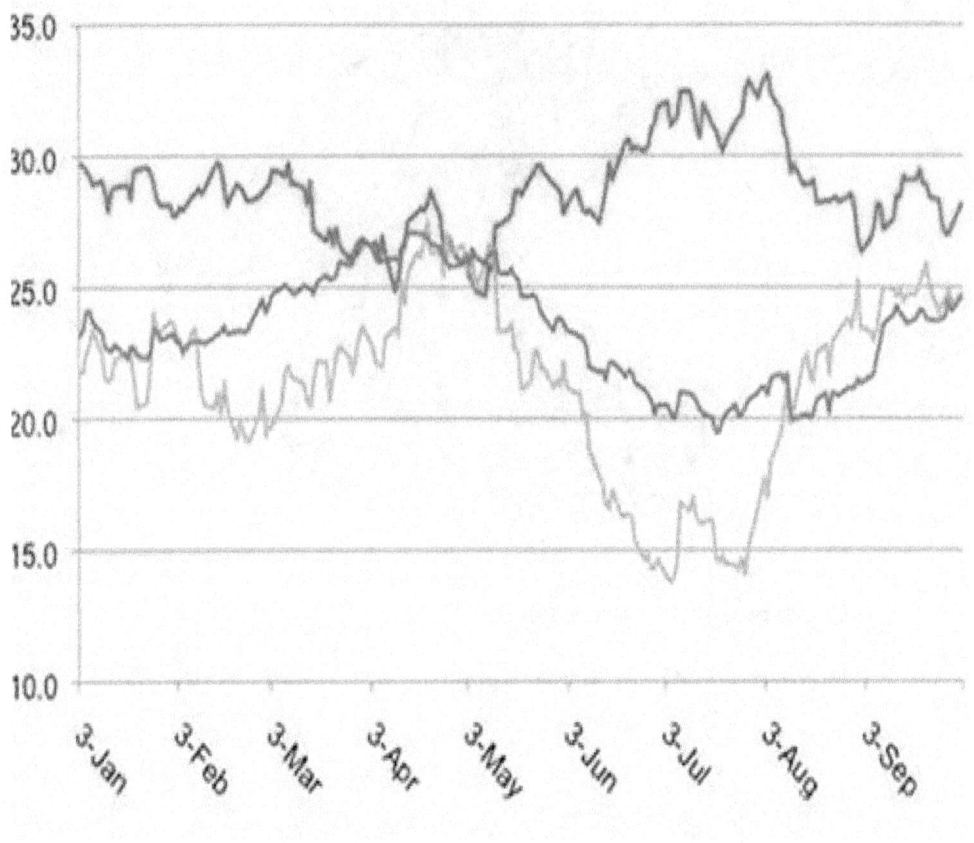

--------- **2013**

----------**2012**

----------**2013**

Stock Price – 2 points

Volatility – 2 points

Total Combined Score – 11 points – 55%

Recommendation; unacceptable – poor stock performance and low international market share

Yinlu

Sales

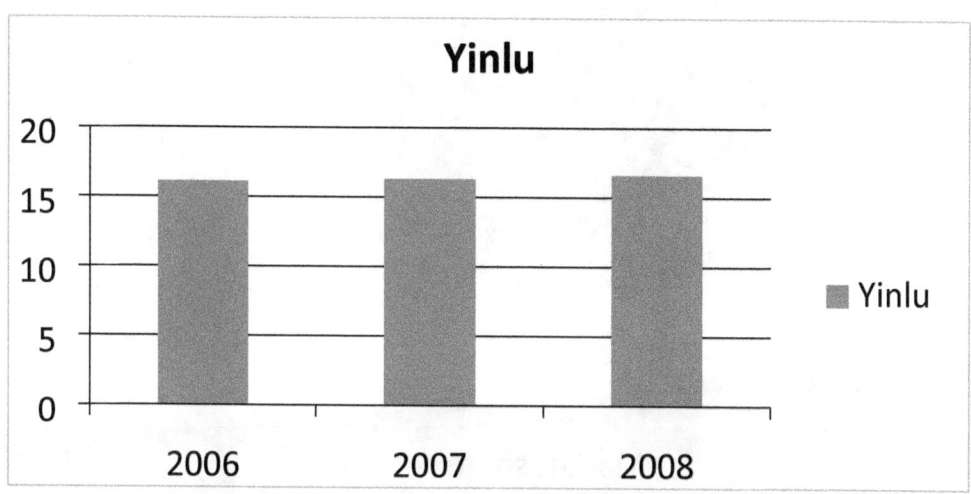

Domestic Sales – 3 points

International Sales – 0 points

Market Share

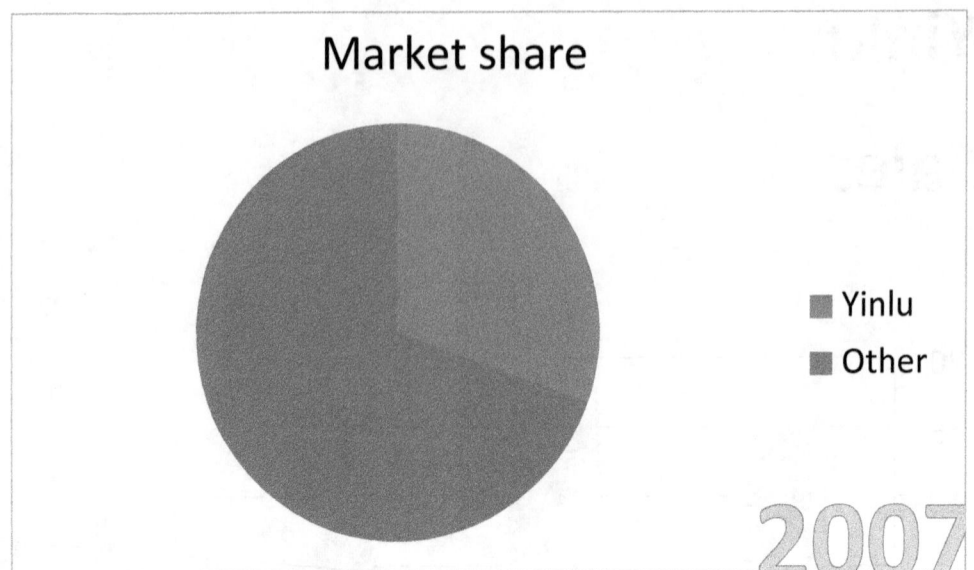

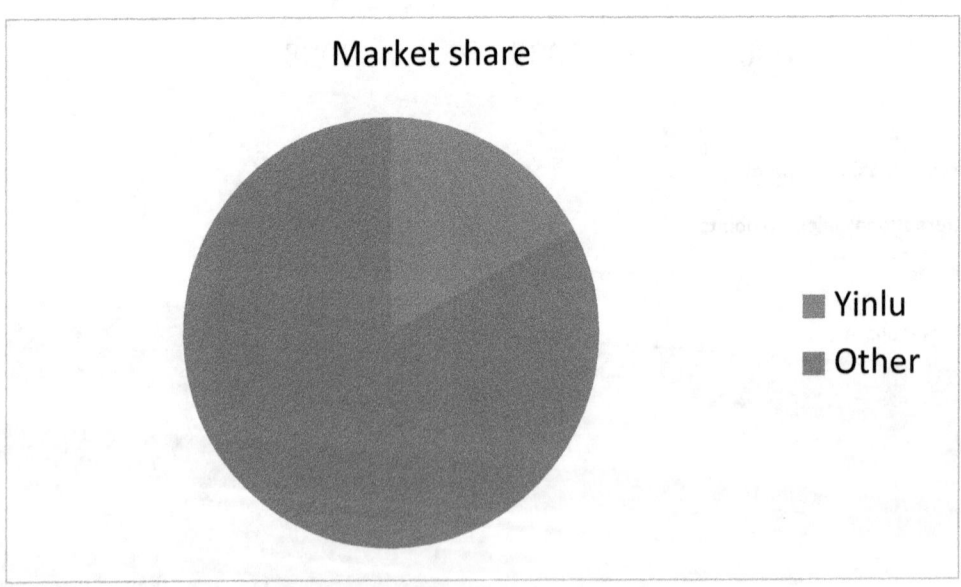

Domestic Market share – 0 points

International Market share – 0 points

Stock Price

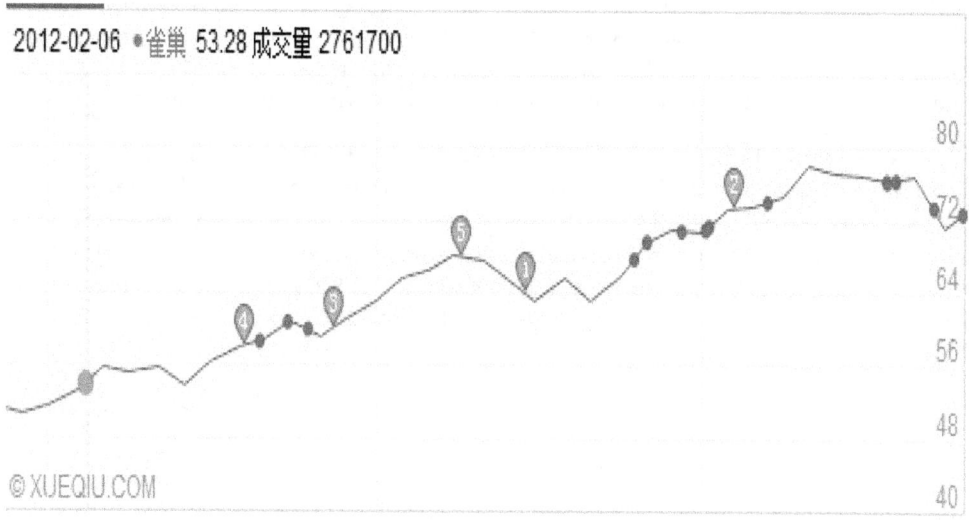

Stock price – 3 points

Volatility – 3 points

Total Combined Score – 9 points – 45%

Recommendation – Unacceptable; no international market share; poor domestic sales. How stock is up in this situation is something Houdini might be interested in.

Summation: As we can see, the vast majority of Chinese companies suffer from the same malady; insufficient market share in the international sales arena. Several have excellent results in the domestic sales arena, and several have fine stock performance based on those domestic sales. But international companies listed on NASDAQ and the NYSE generally have competitive market share in the international arena. So Chinese stocks, on the whole, do not qualify for listing on major stock exchanges.

Several Chinese stocks have unexplainable declines despite impressive sales figures and increasing market shares. This has no basis for economic sense. The only conclusion one can come to about companies like these (Chinese banks, phone companies and others) is that they are state-owned enterprises that show only the sales, but not all of the actual expenses involved with the company. Whether they are state-owned or private is really not paramount; what is important is that the stock performance should accurately reflect the increases in sales and market share. Unfortunately, this is not the case in several Chinese companies that report increases in sales and market share.

www.ingramcontent.com/pod-product-compliance
Lightning Source LLC
Chambersburg PA
CBHW051804170526
45167CB00005B/1878